QUEEN ELIZABETH
The Queen Mother

The Country Life Book of
QUEEN ELIZABETH
The Queen Mother

Godfrey Talbot

Foreword by
HRH The Prince of Wales
KG, KT, PC, GCB

New and Revised Edition

COUNTRY LIFE BOOKS

The photographs appearing on the jacket and the
frontispiece were taken by gracious permission of
Her Majesty Queen Elizabeth The Queen Mother
for Country Life Books by Michael Plomer.

COUNTRY · LIFE
NEWNES·BOOKS

Newnes, itself founded in 1881, purchased
Country Life magazine in 1897. Books were an
important part of the business and more than
eight hundred titles were published prior to
1947. Today Country Life books are published
on many subjects including Architecture,
Natural History, British Heritage, Antiques and
Equestrian sport. Some, such as the Dictionary
of English Furniture, first published in 1924, are
still in print. Sister imprints include Collingridge
and Temple Press Books.

Published by Country Life Books,
an imprint of Newnes Books,
Astronaut House, Feltham, Middlesex, England
and distributed for them by
The Hamlyn Publishing Group Limited
Rushden, Northants, England.

First published 1978
New and revised edition 1983

ISBN 0 600 36861 0

Printed and bound in Italy

Contents

BUCKINGHAM PALACE

Perhaps one of the most difficult things anyone can be asked to do is to write the foreword to a book about their grandmother. I can only admit from the very start that I am hopelessly biased and completely partisan, so that anyone expecting a "balanced" introduction to this book should either put it down at once or turn the page with suitable rapidity.

On the other hand, however many pages they turn over they will probably very quickly discover that the author of this book is equally and unashamedly partisan in his approach to his subject! But I don't think it will make any difference at all, for I suspect that the vast majority of people who acquire this book will have equally partisan views and will therefore have already fallen under the spell of the sparkling, fascinating lady to whom this book is devoted.

I would have said that most grandsons probably have a rather special relationship with their grandmothers, which is no doubt something to do with the difference in generations, but ever since I can remember my grandmother has been the most wonderful example of fun, laughter, warmth, infinite security and, above all else, exquisite taste in so many things. For me, she has always been one of those extraordinarily rare people whose touch can turn everything to gold - whether it be putting people at their ease, turning something dull into something amusing, bringing happiness and comfort to people by her presence or making any house she lives in a unique haven of cosiness and character. She belongs to that priceless brand of human beings whose greatest gift is to enhance life for others through her own effervescent enthusiasm for life. She has been doing that for very nearly 83 years, through war and peace, through change and uncertainty - an inspiration and a figure of love and affection for young and old alike.

You only have to look at the pictures in this book to see what an impact she has made on her century.

CHAPTER I

A Story Afresh

THERE WAS a party in the Palace, an early evening reception. Suddenly the sound of a loud engine clattered from the garden. Some guests were startled and, sherry in hand, went anxiously to the windows. As they did so, it was noticeable that the host at the party, the Queen, was paying no attention to the commotion outside. The cognoscenti among the company also ignored it and whispered: 'The Queen is well used to this. Probably it's her mother coming home from an engagement.'

What the curious guests saw through the windows was a big red helicopter which had landed on the lawn. A smiling lady in a flowered dress was stepping briskly from the machine, ready to pop down to her own Clarence House which is nearby along The Mall.

The grass of Buckingham Palace does in fact quite often make a convenient royal helicopter pad; and that evening's vision of energy who emerged from the aircraft was indeed the fabulous octogenarian whose name is Her Majesty Queen Elizabeth The Queen Mother. The arrival was just one glimpse of a still zestful lady who continues from time to time (despite possible hazard – and an account of one emergency landing is given later in this book) to hop confidently in and out of 'choppers' as she carries out official journeys. It is as natural a form of transport to her as car or train. Admirably old-fashioned in some of her sparkling style and in her beautiful manners though she may be, this Queen is as modern and progressive as ever she was in the business of getting about. She is just as up-to-date in her travelling as any of her descendants. A peerless person. An ageless one, too, it always seems.

The fierce light which beats upon the Throne, an effulgence disclosing almost all the Royal Family in our searching Television Age, has lately put other figures in the centre of the stage and the public's awareness. They are – principally and rightly – the reigning Sovereign herself, Elizabeth II, and then her eldest son and heir, the Prince of Wales, the enchanting new Princess, and their firstborn son, the infant Prince William of Wales who is second in line to the Throne.

Yet the world's interest in the senior figure of them all, the Queen Mother, has not diminished. On the contrary, as she is seen now, in the Eighties, to be still vigorously serving her country and her ideals, she is more than ever lapped in a warmth of public affection wherever she goes.

'Happy Birthday, Queen Mum!' was the shout at the Clarence House gate on August 4, 1980. Her Majesty was eighty years old, and when she appeared, with her daughters, children broke from the crowds to press flowers into her hands.

For as long as most people can remember, she has been a unique star of Britain's First Family. It is sixty years since she became daughter-in-law of a king, George V, forty-six since the start of that dauntless era at her husband's side as Queen Consort of George VI, and over thirty years since her emergence into her present life as Queen Mother for which the nation and the Commonwealth now know and love her best. 'Everybody's Queen Mum' has become an accolade. To the modern generation she seems always to have been exactly that – an institution, no less. Reassuringly on duty.

She is the quintessence of royalty, yet to meet her is to be captivated – not so much perhaps by her grace and good taste, or the chiffons and velvets and the pearls, as by the smile and the melting welcome of the unpretentious human being inside the modes. She can be fallible as well as formidable. She will laugh at her own foibles. She loves to laugh. She is grand, but she is also great fun. Possessed of a talent for public appearance, she genuinely likes meeting people. Her main business is doing just that: taking a helpful interest in as many as possible of activities which British people care about.

So it is an industrious and glowing personality that she gives, and has for so long given, to the twentieth century whose years and her own number the same. She glides now, through the Eighties, with her light shining as brightly as it did long ago when she became royal and began making royalty acceptable and enjoyed. She is respected even by people who protest that monarchy is an anachronism and a bore.

This book is a celebration of Her Majesty – 'The Queen Mother' to the world and in the text of the following pages. That title is the popular one and it avoids confusion with her reigning daughter who bears the same Christian name. But she is also referred to as 'Queen Elizabeth', for that is what she is called by her family and those who serve her.

Her story, a golden thread in the pattern of our times, was long and full when I first wrote the Country Life book about her in 1978. Since then, the book has gone through reprint after reprint. Now the need has come for a new edition – not merely a new impression but an up-to-date perspective with major additions to both words and illustrations. The need is born of the fascinating events of the last five years in the life of this indefatigable Queen: the enormous number of her engagements at home and abroad, her ever-memorable Eightieth Birthday, the joy of her First Grandson's world-watched wedding in the following year, and in 1982 the birth and christening of William Arthur Philip Louis, that special third great-grandchild.

The account of Queen Elizabeth's life, from the start, is still

Opposite, top *Inquiring but unperturbed, the Queen Mother walks from her helicopter after a forced landing soon after take-off in Windsor Great Park. See the story on page 166.*

Opposite, bottom *Walking through St Paul's Cathedral – the Queen one step behind her mother on this occasion – the Eightieth Birthday Thanksgiving Service on July 15, 1980.*

Left *Queen Elizabeth showing her intuitive knack for enjoying being with people and making them feel at ease.*

Below *The scene in St Paul's Cathedral during the Thanksgiving Service on Silver Jubilee Day, June 7, 1977. Seated beside the Queen Mother on this earlier great occasion are Prince Andrew and Prince Edward.*

here in this new edition. The romance and drama of Elizabeth of Glamis is undimmed, the eventful years in which she grew up and emerged from her Scottish family to marry the self-effacing Prince 'Bertie' and become a Royal Duchess. Not many years later we came to know her as the finest Queen Consort in our history. Two World Wars are in the fabric of the story. After the second war came the grievous loss of a husband who was but fifty-six years old – a death which might have sent his widow prematurely to the rocking-chair of retirement in her desolation, but which in fact made Her Majesty, steeling herself, determined to continue on her own the work which an exemplary man and wife had undertaken together.

Fondly, to this day, she speaks of 'the King and I'. Proudly, still, her homeland is 'Our Beloved Country'. Sincerely, she reviews the challenge and change of the years, and – in the words she gave to Parliament when she had achieved eight decades – she has 'always been helped and uplifted by the love of my family, the loyalty and understanding of our people and by my faith in Almighty God.'

The words have the true ring of the character of this leading lady who so far has experienced a full three decades of her 'third life', the Queen Mother years. Happily, her impact is effervescent in a great variety of spheres: scholastic and sporting, social welfare and stage, music and art, community service and cultivation of gardens. She has her regiments and her hospitals, a host of active patronages all benefitting by her interest and enthusiasm. A bare list of them would fill many sheets.

The new pages – the new whole chapters – of this expanded edition of our book have a rich five years to present. Years fresh in the memory, years which have brought new peaks of achievement and acclaim. Years of enduring history.

We cover the twelve months of celebrations which saluted The Birthday in 1980, and much else before and after that. In 1979, for instance, the historic Cinque Ports of the 'invasion coast' of South-East England honoured the royal champion's conspicuous service to the Crown by installing her with great ceremony as their Lord Warden and Admiral. This unique office, though honorary now, was in olden days a command of vital importance, and Winston Churchill was one of those who was proud to occupy the post in the twentieth century. In the long ages of this country's maritime greatness the post meant Guardian and Defender of the ports, and their fleets, which were bulwarks of the Realm. By that measure alone, and by the fact that no woman had ever been Lord Warden before, the appointment was signal acknowledgment of Her Majesty's suitability and stature.

However the transcendent event in the most recent epoch of Queen Elizabeth's life, and a major milepost, too, along the road of the Windsor dynasty, was the marriage on July 29, 1981, of Charles, Prince of Wales, Heir to the Throne – the grandson with whom the Golden Lady of Clarence House has always had a special rapport. That the union was, patently, a love-match made for perfect bliss. And the fact, moreover, that Diana Spencer, Charles's choice – now a Princess, a mother and a Queen Consort-to-be – was a lovely young English girl known and liked by Queen Elizabeth triggered explosions of happiness in Her Majesty's house on the February day when the official announcement of betrothal was issued.

For *two* grandmothers heard the news together. The nineteen-year-old Lady Diana, as the Princess of Wales was then, is a granddaughter of Ruth, the Dowager Lady Fermoy,

who has been a close friend of the Queen Mother since her marriage and for twenty-five years a senior lady-in-waiting to her. Now it happened that Lady Fermoy was on duty at Her Majesty's London home on Engagement Day.

Small wonder then that, whilst no Buckingham Palace party or balcony appearance by the Prince and his fiancée took place that evening, there was, on the contrary, simply a small and quite private dinner at Clarence House. Two starry-eyed young people and two scintillating grannies. The celebration evening was very personal, neither photographed nor reported. But one can imagine that the betrothal which had been made public that day was something greatly hoped-for, perhaps planned-for, at Clarence House. It is difficult to resist conjuring up a picture of the special joy registered on the faces of those two grandmothers.

The Royal Wedding was a dazzling light in a dark world – and a sumptuous story for this book. The euphoria of it all had scarcely waned when public excitement was rekindled at the news that a child was on the way. The arrival of the baby Prince William, in the midsummer of 1982 and just ten days before his mother's twenty-first birthday, then caused waves of extra-ordinary delight.

Delight for a world eager to embrace romance and motherhood and a healthy newcomer to his special realm. Delight for the British Monarchy, the royal House. Particular public delight in the young mother, for the country had been in love with the new Princess of Wales from the start. She was something to rejoice about: a tall and tender girl, once unknown but now royal, yet as appealingly fresh and free in honest style as ever she was in the sweater-and-jeans days of kinder-garten-teacher Diana. Here she was, nevertheless, a Princess to the manner born, smiling with quiet pride, promptly producing a son – and, by so doing, producing a straight-forward prospect of monarchial continuity. Her Royal Highness, this new and invigorating star in the galaxy of the Royal Family, is remarkable in her own right. There is bright precedent for her impact upon the scene.

Historians of the future, recalling how today's Queen Mother, when *she* was young, stepped lightsomely down from

Scotland into the Royal Family and began to transform it sixty years ago, may well compare *her* arrival to the entry into the Family of the Princess of Wales we possess now. For Lady Elizabeth Bowes-Lyon and Lady Diana Spencer, both of them assets to the Monarchy although they are two generations apart, have character and effect in common. Each in her time has on marriage, by her refreshing nature, brought enrichment and salutary change into the House of Windsor from a world outside palace walls. Brisk air and sunshine entered with them: high spirits, high standards, and a love of family life. Neither was born a princess, yet each was close enough to royalty to know and accept the pressures, as well as the privileges, of the estate they had entered.

In presenting this new and up-to-date story of Queen Elizabeth The Queen Mother – a story with additional illustrations, many of them exclusive and in colour – writer and publishers have been fortunate in help from many sources. The gracious permission of the Queen was given for the reproduction of a number of her pictures and for photography at palaces and castles – places that are *homes*, not monuments. There is a natural emphasis not only on royal Deeside but on Royal Lodge, Windsor, and on Clarence House, London, for they have been long identified with this Mother of the Sovereign.

Above all, Her Majesty The Queen Mother herself has with great kindness co-operated in the making of the book (not that it is a dictated or censored tale: the opinions, and any errors, are the author's). Her own practical assistance, and that of her Household, in giving factual information and facilities, have once more been invaluable. A series of new photographs taken at Clarence House, expressly for this publication, has been a privilege enjoyed. A measure of the royal help and personal interest was that after Prince William's christening and the celebrations attending it – on Queen Elizabeth's eighty-second birthday – Her Majesty made time before departure for her Scottish summer to put herself and her house and garden at the disposal of publisher and photographer. For that thoughtfulness, the very pictures add their thanks.

The wealth of illustration in this Country Life book was a

Opposite The smile from mother to daughter as the Queen Mother and the Queen take their seats in St Paul's for the historic Eightieth Year Service.

Above Birthday Thanksgiving pageantry in July 1980 as Her Majesty rides in a Sovereign's procession to the Cathedral. The Prince of Wales is with her.

great attraction from the moment the original edition was published. Many of the photographs are retained in this revised edition because of their historical importance and, in many cases, their uniqueness – and because they lead naturally to what had been added: the richly picturesque events of the most recent five years.

It is an honour to carry again a Foreword written by the Heir to the Throne, pronouncing a grandson's boundless regard for Queen Elizabeth. The Prince of Wales's memorable words now salute *eighty-three* years of an inspiring life, and the impact of those years upon this century.

It would be pleasant and proper to express thanks to *all* who have generously given of their time and knowledge to make the book authentic and attractive, but many helpers have asked for anonymity. Nevertheless, special gratitude must be set down to Lieutenant-Colonel Sir Martin Gilliat, GCVO, MBE, LL.D., Private Secretary to The Queen Mother; and to Captain Alastair Aird, CVO, Comptroller of Her Majesty's Household. Major John Griffin, CVO, Press Secretary at Clarence House, has been unremitting in help. Thanks also are due to Lord Adam Gordon, KCVO, MBE; the Hon. Lady Bowes-Lyon; Sir Robin Mackworth-Young, KCVO, FSA, Librarian and Assistant Keeper of The Queen's Archives at Windsor Castle; Sir Douglas Logan, former Principal of the University of London; the seventeenth Earl of Strathmore and Kinghorne at Glamis Castle; Squadron Leader Sir David Checketts, KCVO, former Private Secretary to the Prince of Wales; and Ronald Allison, CVO, former Press Secretary at Buckingham Palace.

Particular thanks to my publisher, Robert Owen, Editorial Director of Country Life Books, who in the making of this volume has laboured well beyond the letter of the law.

And now to the story.

CHAPTER 2

From Scotland with Love

THE GIRL who was to become a Queen unique in history and Britain's last Empress was born on August 4, 1900. At that time, Queen Victoria was dying – worn out by her sheer old age and her fretting over a Boer War that seemed endless. But the baby Elizabeth Bowes-Lyon had no connection with the crown or the conflict; she was not a princess and did not come from a palace; and the newspapers had little space to record the secluded arrival of the ninth child of the Strathmores, a noble though happily unpretentious Scots family – even though the great Castle of Glamis was one of their homes.

She was born in England but is rightly regarded as a Scotswoman and has royal blood of her own Northern Realm in her veins. Her pedigree is not only as distinguished, but also as dramatic, as anything in the history of the *English* Throne. The

Opposite *Glamis Castle, the Queen Mother's girlhood home.*

Below *Lord and Lady Strathmore with their children. Lady Elizabeth, a small girl, stands by her mother.*

family tale is no cosy chronicle. One of her female forebears, for instance, was burned as a witch – an event which took place in the period when Shakespeare was bubbling his own cauldron of sorcery in the writings of *Macbeth*, portraying King Duncan's murderer as the Thane of Glamis.

Robert the Bruce, King of Scotland, was one of Queen Elizabeth's ancestors. But there is also a Welsh strain. Dig wide and deep enough into her genealogy and up comes one of the most famous of Welshmen, for she can trace one of her lines of descent from the awesome warrior chief Owain, 'the wild and irregular Glendwr', last hero of the independent Princes. No wonder the lady has those eyes of Celtic summer-blue.

The English are in her family history too: Smiths and Brownes only a few generations back. Even American ancestry can be found, with General Robert E. Lee and George Washington himself there, by way of relatives of Smiths into which one of her family married in the nineteenth century. For, two centuries earlier than that, some of the Smith predecessors

had emigrated during the brief Cromwellian interlude which denied England her kings, and had put down distinguished roots in Virginia. However, our story is concerned mainly with the eastern side of the Atlantic.

Though she was born in England of an English mother, the Scottish part of the Queen Mother's background is the one which matters most. It is a long and exciting tapestry, for certain of the Strathmores of past ages married picturesque rogues. Despite this, the record of the Bowes-Lyon dynasty presents a picture of fine, public-spirited people.

The family have owned Glamis Castle, twelve miles north of Dundee, since the fourteenth century, when it came to them through Princess Joan, daughter of King Robert II; she married the tall Sir John Lyon, Keeper of the Privy Seal, called 'The White Lyon' because of his fair hair. It is from this union that Queen Elizabeth is directly descended. Sir John, on that marriage into Scotland's royal family, became the Thane, the first Lord Glamis, and acquired the lands which attended the title. Property he had, but probably no great inherited wealth. Money arrived in the family much later, considerably after the Earldom of Strathmore and Kinghorne had been bestowed in Stuart times.

Affluence enters the story, in fact, in the middle of the eighteenth century when the nineteenth Lord Glamis (ninth Earl of Strathmore) married a certain Miss Eleanor Bowes, who was the only child and heiress of George Bowes, a wealthy industrialist in County Durham. He transferred all his fortune and all his estates, in the North and in Hertfordshire, through his daughter, to the Lyon family on condition that they changed their surname to Bowes. This they did, but after the magnate died they brought the old name smartly back. For a time they paid titular tribute to the dowry by calling themselves Lyon-Bowes before adopting the present style of Bowes-Lyon, the change being made by the thirteenth Earl of Strathmore, our present Queen Mother's paternal grandfather.

Not that the old Bowes side of the family should be thought of as unlettered mineowners and little more. There were men of taste. John Bowes, a capitalist of culture, left behind at the end of the last century an extraordinary architectural monument and treasure house in the North of England. He and his French wife, an artist, collected paintings, furniture and ceramics in profusion, and this rich heritage is today assembled in all its magnificence in the Bowes Museum near the town of Barnard Castle. The building itself, an astonishing sight to find at the edge of the remote Durham moorlands, is a massive French château crammed with priceless exhibits from all over Europe and open for everyone to see. It is a legacy characteristic of the enduring Bowes-Lyon urge to serve the public.

We must come much further down the map of Britain to locate the beginning of Queen Elizabeth The Queen Mother's own life story: further down than Angus and further down than Durham. The story starts in the South of England. The Hon. Elizabeth Angela Marguerite Bowes-Lyon was born in London – her parents had a house in Mayfair – but from the very first days of her life her home was the family's country place in Hertfordshire, St Paul's Walden Bury, a rambling red-brick, largely Georgian house which proved to be a most delightful jumble of a home, rich in old outbuildings and lovely gardens – bliss for young children to grow up in. (The baby's father must have been singularly attached to the house, for when he officially logged Elizabeth's arrival – the birth certificate landed

at the Registrar's office in nearby Hitchin on September 21, over six weeks late and only two days before the christening – the entry gave St Paul's as the birth*place*. So does a plaque in the local church: the All Saints parish claims birth as well as baptism.) The exact location of the birth seems lost in the mists of time.

She was the youngest but one – and today is the only survivor – of the ten children of Lord and Lady Glamis. Her father inherited the title of fourteenth Earl of Strathmore when she was three, and thus she inherited the courtesy title of Lady Elizabeth. Soon after her came David, last child of that large and close-knit family, the David whom she always specially loved. The girl and boy were inseparable companions – for the other children were much older – Elizabeth was an aunt at ten. In fact they grew up through childhood like twins. Their mother used to call them 'my two Benjamins', and admitted that such was the gap in age between them and the rest of the family that people mistook them for her grandchildren.

Elizabeth's father in later life was made Lord Lieutenant of the county of Angus. But he was a quiet, devout, rather retiring and old-fashioned country gentleman, kindly and affectionate. He had some pride in his silky moustache, which he used to part before kissing a child. An unobtrusive and modest man. Somehow it was characteristic that he made his own drink for breakfast – cocoa.

It was her mother, the Countess of Strathmore, who was the memorably shining figure, shaping the life of a blithe and uninhibited family. Formerly Miss Nina Cavendish-Bentinck, a kinswoman of the Dukes of Portland, she was a lady of strong yet sweet personality, serene to the point of casualness, hardworking and easygoing at the same time, naturally artistic, musically talented, a knowledgeable botanist and brilliant gardener. An adored mother, inspiring the children at whatever they were engaged upon. And a dynamo of enthusiasm and example. 'Life is for living and working at', she used to say. 'If you find anything or anybody a bore, the fault is in yourself.'

There was nothing boring at St Paul's Walden Bury, where the small Elizabeth spent much of her time in the sunlit Edwardian years. Life was warm and busy and free in the old house. Lessons were to be learned in the nursery where the big fireguard and the rocking-horse stood and where the bookshelves and the fascinating dressing-up chest full of period costumes beckoned. And there were plenty of places to escape to: friendly stillroom, kitchen, brew-house, attic and, outside, in the fields and stable beside the flower gardens and gladed treelands, were to be found old Bobs the Shetland pony, the dogs and chickens, pigeons and ring-doves, the kittens and the tortoises. Even the statues in the grounds were friends: the Discus Thrower was called by the children the Running Footman or the Bounding Butler. St Paul's was a marvellous place for the imaginative games of Elizabeth and David. The woods, the shrubberies, the ponds and carpets of anemones – they were all enchantment. It was there that the Queen Mother's love of country gardens was first instilled.

It was also there – and indeed wherever the family were living – that Elizabeth and David grew up and had their character moulded under the firm influence of a 'most wonderful woman' (the late Sir David Bowes-Lyon's description) called Clara Knight, their nurse, always known as 'Allah' because when they were tiny that name was the nearest they could get to pronouncing Clara. Allah was the finest of the old type of nanny,

Right *At the back of St Paul's Walden Bury, today the home of the Hon. Lady Bowes-Lyon; looking down on the barns and granary is the old clock tower, and belfry – a sight which must have been very familiar in childhood to Lady Elizabeth as she played in the gardens.*

Below *During the early years of this century the children of the fourteenth Earl and Countess of Strathmore frequently played in and around the barns and pre-sixteenth-century granary (centre).*

Left *Elizabeth, aged four and David, aged three, the youngest of the ten Bowes-Lyon children.*

Opposite *Fine trees and old statuary on the sweep of lawn – a view of St Paul's Walden Bury, some thirty miles north of London.*

Left *Elizabeth and David building a house of cards at their family's country home, St Paul's Walden Bury.*

Left *The Garden Room at St Paul's Walden Bury, more usually known as the Red Room, is today much as it was during the early years of Lady Elizabeth Bowes-Lyon, who lived at the house up to the time of her marriage in 1923.*

Below *In the grounds of St Paul's is this graceful and peaceful temple The architect was Sir William Chambers (1726–96). The temple, which had stood in Dansen Park, Bexley Heath, was brought to St Paul's by Sir David and Lady Bowes-Lyon in 1961.*

quiet, high principled, tenderly strict, utterly professional and loyal, completely in control of her young charges and their paddywhacks, dependable day and night whether parents were at home or away, an unruffled goddess of nursery parties and perambulator parades. She was in the service of the Strathmores all her life; she went off and mothered the little Elphinstones when Elizabeth's eldest sister married Lord Elphinstone and had her own children. In her turn, Elizabeth – who by then was Duchess of York – unhesitatingly stole the guiding paragon of her childhood to look after her own first baby when Princess Elizabeth was born.

Back in those days when Queen Elizabeth was a little girl, the family home and family nursery were as much at Glamis as at St Paul's, for the Strathmores were in Scotland for a good part of every year. Within the bulky stone walls of the turreted Castle the education of the youngest daughter proceeded agreeably under Lady Strathmore's personal supervision and Allah's loving eye. Elizabeth did not go away to school (though there were two terms in early childhood spent at a day school for young ladies in South Audley Street, London). The absorption of English, French, history, music and dancing went steadily forward under the tuition of a succession of governesses and specialist teachers, who found their pupil apt, lively and mischievous.

Much of the schooling was at the Bury, but holidays were usually spent up at Glamis. Elizabeth's spirits never seemed to be cowed by the forbidding gauntness of the great mansion around her. Dark stone stairways and spooky attics were but the perfect playgrounds for hide-and-seek; the antlers and armour and axes round the bare walls only reminders of exciting history. Ghost stories brought a delicious shiver, and the grim legends of many a dark deed through the Castle's violent centuries spiced the childhood hours. Visible reminders of a romantic and turbulent past, carefully preserved, were familiar to the children. A watch of Bonny Prince Charlie's for instance: the Young Pretender had left it ticking beside his bed when the English came after him by night and he had to flee the house in haste. No wonder the children were affected by accounts of ancient battle and siege as they played. One of their games – before David, to his sister's sorrow, went away to school – was 'repelling raiders' by pouring boiling oil down from the turreted roof upon new arrivals at the entrance to the house. The 'oil' was cold water, but shock enough for unsuspecting visitors.

A story is told in Glamis village of one time when Elizabeth's sense of fun exploded in startling fashion. It was one afternoon when, after music instruction, she went on sitting at the harmonium in the Castle chapel. (Her Majesty today remembers 'those awful pedals which you pumped to make the bellows work'.) The small fingers which had been plodding laboriously up and down the keys doing battle with a Handel voluntary suddenly changed tempo and, to the accompaniment of squeaks of laughter from the young organist, the chapel resounded to a spirited version of 'Yip-i-addy-i-ay!'

Most of the occupations and escapades were gentler and more orthodox: sewing, gardening, playing somewhat haphazard tennis and croquet, picnicking in the great park surrounding the house, games of charades in the evenings, and going off to shop occasionally in the village – where there are memories of a bewitching little person with dancing eyes who used to say 'Hello, I'm Elizabeth Lyon.' People on the estate and in the village had the impression that she didn't like the Bowes name

too much. They were, and the whole district still is, quietly possessive about Lady Elizabeth. She may have gone away, she may have houses in London and other parts of Scotland, but she is to them a Scots lassie who belongs to Glamis.

And to the royal lady herself – for all the pull of Deeside and remote Caithness, where today she can walk casually down the main street of the seaport of Thurso and pop in and out of homely shops with no fuss at all, Glamis has remained a part of Scotland that is special and precious. Not often visited now, it is true, for today the royal homes in the Northern Realm mean Balmoral and Birkhall and that outpost, called the Castle of Mey, beside the Pentland Firth, but there must remain for Her Majesty a unique nostalgia for the great picturebook fortress-house in the soft green hills below the Grampian wall – Glamis, setting of the green and golden years of the girl who was to become a Queen.

But in those early years of the century the Strathmore family moved, freely and unpublicized, between North and South from the one house to the other. They were not inclined to be townsfolk. It was in the untramelled, open-air atmosphere of country homes and old-fashioned gardens that Lady Elizabeth Bowes-Lyon lived and laughed and grew up – and passed her Junior Oxford. From time to time there were excursions to London, with David when he was home on holiday from boarding school. And special treats in Town for special occasions.

One of these she will always remember – her fourteenth birthday, for it brought to the world as well as to her a new, and sometimes melancholy, chapter of experience. The day was August 4, 1914, the date on which the Kaiser's War began. Although it was on the very night when the outbreak of hostilities was officially declared, Elizabeth's promised visit to a West End theatre was not cancelled. She sat with her family in a box at the Coliseum, and at the end of the variety performance she looked down on an audience which boiled with sudden excitement and patriotism expressed in wild cheering. At midnight, home in bed in the Strathmores' London house, she could hear the roaring of the crowds going down The Mall and gathering outside Buckingham Palace, calling for George V, for four years their King and now leader of a nation at war. It was a strident start to sombre days.

Then back to the quiet of Glamis, for Elizabeth was to spend most of the First World War years in a castle, as, a quarter of a century later, her daughter, also a Queen-to-be, was to spend the Second-World-War years in another castle, Windsor. Chill and emptiness entered the life of Elizabeth Bowes-Lyon as brothers put on uniform and went away (Fergus to be killed at the battle of Loos in 1915).

Glamis Castle was turned into a convalescent hospital for the wounded; and soon Elizabeth, helping her mother and sisters to run the place, became a very hard-working teenager indeed. Schoolroom routine was maintained, but now there was sterner stuff to do after lessons were over. With grim regularity, as the war ground on and the casualties mounted, ambulances filled with maimed men in khaki and hospital blues came lumbering over the Sidlaw hills. And at Glamis many shattered men found healing and cheer for both body and spirit.

Whatever trepidation the wounded soldiers first felt at the prospect of being organized by a countess in a cold Scottish castle, the fears soon disappeared in the warm ambience of Lady Strathmore's personality and the simple charm of the young

Prince Albert, photographed in 1910 as a cadet at the Royal Naval College, Osborne. In the war years later he saw service as an officer in HMS Collingwood *at the Battle of Jutland.*

Prince 'Bertie' – as the second son was known to the family – a young man of nineteen, on his polo pony at Windsor in 1914.

daughter. The radiant sympathy and tonic spirits of the girl with the fringe and the infectious smile soon had the men competing for her company at mealtimes, soon had them begging her help in writing letters and her high-spirited participation in games of cards. She played the piano and sang with them; she teased them, shopped in the village for them, called them by their Christian names. They were guests in her mother's house, and as junior hostess she was completely natural and at ease in looking after them. In fact those Servicemen who spent their convalescence at Glamis were the first people outside her own family circle to experience at close hand the entrancing character which the wide world was to know in years to come when that girl became a Queen. As one man put it then, and as so many people have said so often since, 'She always made you feel you were the one person in the world she wanted to be seeing. It was great medicine!'

She was eighteen, assured and attractive, when the war ended. She had come to womanhood in anxious and unnatural times, confined and conditioned by four years of emergency. But life had not been all grimness, had not been entirely devoid of the dances and occasional parties she loved. She had become an accomplished hostess, interested in everything around her, never at a loss in conversation, full of fun. Lessons had not been forced, but had come easily: she already spoke French like a native. Vivacity and the social graces were hers, and a no-nonsense will of her own beneath the quiet self-control.

Elizabeth was of course a member of an aristocratic family. She was moreover a pretty girl and a perfect dancer, and when after the end of the war she went south from Glamis once more,

entering the newly hectic Society of the early Twenties in London, she was much in demand. She enjoyed herself very much, though popularity with young men never went to her head and she never sought to tie her beaux. She was not conceited: it was a natural thing to have a string of admirers. People had always been in love with her. She went to dances, visited country houses, attended strawberries-and-cream Ascot. Life was busy and sweet.

Yet the name of this Lady Elizabeth was still unknown to the public in England. She was not, even in small type, in the Court and Social columns of the newspapers. It was her friendship – first of all through Girl Guide work – with Princess Mary, the daughter of King George and later known as the Princess Royal, which began her path to recognition and to royalty. She was invited to the Palace, met the King and Queen Mary, and also met the King's second son, Prince 'Bertie' – Albert, Duke of York. The two had experienced a brief encounter years before at a children's party when Elizabeth was five and Bertie ten; but real acquaintance began only now, and gradually too.

The year was 1920. The Duke of York too was emerging, though with a stiff shyness which was a contrast to Lady Elizabeth's relaxed spontaneity, from the experiences of wartime. The Royal Navy had been his chosen career and, in spite of periods of ill health, he had served at sea as a junior officer and had been at the battle of Jutland. Perseveringly he had then qualified as a pilot in the Royal Air Force and had taken a course in economics at Trinity College, Cambridge. Though quite good-looking, he was far from being an extrovert full of small talk and self-confidence. He envied and admired

Lady Elizabeth and friends ready for a ride. (From the left) Lady Doris Gordon Lennox, Lord Settrington, Lady Elizabeth, the Hon. *Bruce Ogilvy, the Earl of Haddington, Miss Alex Cavendish (seated) and the Hon. Diamond Hardinge.*

people socially at ease and conversationally fluent. He thought Elizabeth Lyon was wonderful.

Happily, this Royal Duke was a friend and shooting companion of the Bowes-Lyon brothers, and occasionally he went to stay at Glamis and also at St Paul's Walden Bury. He loved those visits. The Strathmore family's unsophisticated life style, the unregimented jollity, the tennis with Elizabeth, the evenings joining in old songs round the grand piano – everything was a marvellous contrast to the unrelieved starchiness of the life of the Court in which he had been brought up. King George and Queen Mary were shy and old-fashioned parents, their primness of manner, rendered more pronounced by occasional efforts at forced jocularity, made it difficult for them to communicate with their children, for whom they never gave parties. So the days spent with the welcoming, boisterous Bowes-Lyons must have been almost intoxicatingly sunny for the very nice but very nervous Duke of York, for whom early life had been lonely and painful, bedevilled by self-consciousness and bouts of gloomy temper which stemmed from an intractable stammer. Life with the 'Lyons' was a revelation and a joy.

And the meetings with Lady Elizabeth, even judged by the reports the hesitant Prince gave to his hidebound parents, were stunning. Her effect on him even dispelled some of his hesitancy and had him competing as eagerly as he could with her eternal circle of joyous admirers for the pleasure of a dance. He was in love. He was for two years a suitor, however shyly in the background. He was delighted to be near Elizabeth, hopeful of the possibility of a future with her, when in 1922 she was a bridesmaid at the wedding of Princess Mary.

To Queen Mary it was clear that Elizabeth would make an ideal wife for Bertie. Gruff King George with wisdom and truth declared, 'You'll be a lucky feller if she accepts you.'

The feller had to wait, and he was not altogether patient about it. But it was not the easiest thing in the world for the happy and sought-after girl to make her decision. Warmth and affection in her went out to Bertie. There was much that appealed: his modesty and honesty, his kindness and his self-effacing manners and his high standards, the patent goodness and devotion of him. Yet she hesitated. To say yes would be to step out of her private world and the glow of an adorably informal family into not only the harsh limelight of public life and work, but also into a Court circle of royal routine much more cold and isolated than anything practised by the British Monarchy today.

But the Duke of York had fortitude and a steady persistence in pressing his suit. And at last he was rewarded. She accepted. He had won her heart. One Sunday morning early in 1923, as they walked together through the St Paul's woodlands which had been the fairy playgrounds of Elizabeth's childhood, Prince Bertie, twenty-seven years old, proposed to the girl of his dreams, who was twenty-two then, and received the answer he had longed for. He dispatched, in code, a joyful telegram to the King and Queen at Sandringham; and three days later the Court Circular announced the betrothal.

The engagement came unheralded upon the public. Popular though she had become in the country houses and the Society circles in which she had moved, this Lady Elizabeth was not then widely known. The newspapers scrambled not very

successfully for details about her, and the betrothal reports were short. Nor was the St Paul's house overwhelmed by Fleet Street photographers. The climate of publicity was not feverish in those days: in any case, although here was the first of the King's sons to become affianced, it was not this one but the eldest son, the Heir, who compelled journalistic attention. Press and public continued to concentrate on the debonair and dashing David, the Prince of Wales, who had no inferiority complex and one day would be King. Even so, inevitably the reporters began to scrutinize and gently publicize the Lady who was to marry the second Prince; readers discovered that she was pretty and witty, intriguingly tender too. Well brought up, of course, nicely reserved and composed, yet at the same time charmingly impulsive and direct. Much more than just an upper-class beauty.

As to the Lady's family, it was typical of the Bowes-Lyons that they were not concerned that their Elizabeth was making a fine match. They were simply glad that she was marrying a good man for whom they had formed such liking.

The engagement was short and the wedding took place in Westminster Abbey on April 26, 1923. The groom's brothers, the Prince of Wales and Prince Henry, were his supporters, and Lady Elizabeth had eight bridesmaids. White roses of York and white heather of Scotland were in the bride's bouquet as she set off to church from her father's house, now in Bruton Street, Mayfair. Few brides, however, can have held their wedding day flowers in hand for so short a time, for, once inside the Abbey, Lady Elizabeth spontaneously laid her bouquet on the tomb of the Unknown Warrior at the West Door – and walked to the altar without it.

After the service, the London streets showered confetti and the bands played Highland airs. It rained, but the crowds were enormous and enthusiastic. The marriage was as popular as would be the weddings of that bride's elder daughter and granddaughter (Elizabeth II and Princess Anne) twenty-four and fifty years later – and without broadcasting too: an obscurantist Abbey Chapter, horrified at the idea of radio coverage of the service, refused the BBC's request to put the

wedding on the new 'wireless'. Direct commentary and a relay of a royal wedding had never been allowed: there was a fear that 'disrespectful people might hear it whilst sitting in public houses with their hats on.' (Even in 1947 when Princess Elizabeth married Prince Philip, although the microphones of 'the wireless' had by then become established in the Abbey, the newfangled medium of television, restricted to filming, got in only after much pleading and negotiation – a very different state of affairs from what we have come to expect nowadays when royal occasions at Westminster and St Paul's Cathedral have become Television Spectaculars.)

So in 1923 Elizabeth of Glamis became a Duchess and a Royal Highness. The King formally conferred the dignity of a Princess upon her during the wedding breakfast, at which the bride needed all her strength and much help from her husband, to saw the first incision into a wedding cake nine feet high.

The honeymoon was spent at Polesden Lacey in Surrey, then the spacious country house of Mrs Ronald Greville, and at Glamis, where the weather was bleakly uncivil and Her Royal Highness unromantically developed whooping cough.

From her first entry into royal life, the new Duchess found herself the object of much public inspection. Without ostentation, she carried her new rank as though born to it, taking the Press attention naturally, with pleasure and also with modest surprise. She was, as she was always to be, courteous and helpful to reporters. Once, indeed, her father-in-law, the King, thought she had been a little too informal and informative about herself and Prince Bertie to a journalist who called on her; His Majesty sent an equerry round to Bruton Street to ask that there should be no interviews. George V had fixed ideas, rooted in the past,

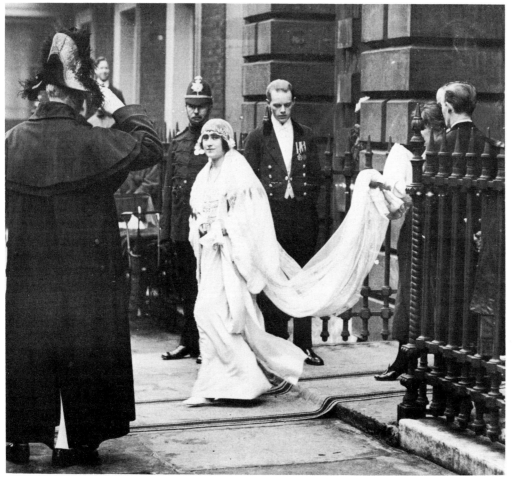

Top *The official engagement picture of Lady Elizabeth and her fiancé, the Prince 'Bertie' who had become HRH the Duke of York.*

Left *Lady Elizabeth Bowes-Lyon leaving her parents' London home in Bruton Street for her marriage to the Duke of York in Westminster Abbey.*

Left *The official wedding photograph of Their Royal Highnesses the Duke and Duchess of York, April 26, 1923.*

Below *On their honeymoon the Duke and Duchess are seen leaving church after the morning service at Bookham, Surrey on April 29, 1923.*

Above *Golf at Polesden Lacey, where the first part of the honeymoon was spent.*

Left *Queen Mary with the Duke and Duchess of York and Prince George, later the Duke of Kent, at Balmoral in September 1923.*

Opposite *The Yorks leaving Bruton Street for the 1927 tour of Australia and New Zealand. They would not see their infant daughter for another six months.*

Above *The Duke and Duchess of York opening the Federal Parliament of Australia in Canberra during their antipodean journey. The tour was the Duke's first major test in public duty.*

on almost everything, certainly on what ladies should do and also what they should wear. New styles, men's and women's, infuriated him. In his own clothes he stuck to the fashions of his youth, continuing to appear in hard hats, trousers creased at the sides, spats and cloth-topped boots to the end of his life in the mid-Thirties. He seemed at war with the twentieth century.

All the same, the King was captivated by his lively daughter-in-law; he quickened to her refreshing spirit just as the normally undemonstrative Queen Mary had done from the first. He relaxed for her the Palace's notoriously strict rules about punctuality, and, to the family's astonishment – for they always had to be at table and ready to start meals absolutely 'on the dot' – he merely smiled when one day she arrived for dinner late and apologetic. 'Not at all, my dear,' he said. 'We must have sat down a few minutes too early.' She had a natural rapport with him, warmer than anything which existed between the Monarch and his own offspring. The Duchess instinctively understood his need of orderliness and his respect for custom and tradition – and in this she was the antithesis of her brother-in-law, the Prince of Wales, who found himself in an almost

perpetual state of suppressed rebellion against a tetchy and censorious parent.

The newly married second son, the Duke of York, though jumpy under his father's quarter-deck manner, had no such conflict: he shared many of the King's ideas about duty and custom, and in any case he was now happily out of the family nest. Life with Elizabeth brought to him a hitherto unknown atmosphere of content and affection. He had an adored partner to share his public engagements. He marvelled at the way she sailed through public duties on her own. She laid a foundation stone and made a speech as though it was the most exciting way of spending an afternoon that she could imagine.

Above all, she began to give to her husband the loving sympathy and practical help he so needed with the task of making *his* speeches. It was agony at that time for the Duke to say even a few words in public, such was the impediment from which he suffered. The trouble was a hesitation, an inability to pronounce, for instance, the initial hard consonants of certain words. (Thus he would always say 'Their Majesties' instead of 'the King and Queen'.) The Duchess encouraged him to rehearse what he had to say, and to relax more when he was on his feet and making the speeches. She refused to believe that his hesitation of speech was incurable, and later on she persuaded her husband to consult an Australian expert in speech defects, Lionel Logue, who was practising in Harley Street. Fortunately the Duke got on well with Mr Logue as an individual, and so he tried very hard to respond to his treatment. The Logue therapy was to get his patient to breathe in a new way, consciously making his diaphragm work when he talked; and signs of hopeful results began to show after weeks of daily exercise at this

Opposite, top *The royal couple wave farewell to the crowd at Maitland, New South Wales.*

Opposite, bottom *During the stop in Fiji in February 1927, Ratu Popi E. Seniloli, the grandson of King Cakodau, presented the Duke of York with a 'Tabua', a whale's tooth, traditional symbol of homage and affection.*

Above *The scene at Guildhall in 1927, when the Duke of York received the Freedom of the City of London. On the right are the Prince of Wales (later Edward VIII) and the Dukes of Kent and Connaught.*

Right *Princess Elizabeth is circled by her proud parents and by the grandparents, King George V and Queen Mary on the left and the Earl and Countess of Strathmore on the right.*

method. The fact that in his new life as a married man the Duke
was less gloomy and withdrawn also helped. And so did the
travels which he and the Duchess embarked upon.

The Duchess suffered from bronchitis during the first winter
of her marriage, and so in the second winter of 1924–5, her
husband obtained the King's permission to take her for a few
weeks into the sunshine of East Africa. The arranged programme included some official engagements, but mainly
consisted of camping, sightseeing in country areas, and game
hunting. The health and strength of both the travellers
benefitted from the safari. They enjoyed the rough tent life in
the reserves and forests, the meetings with tribal chiefs, and the
treks and explorations of rivers more than the cushioned
receptions and soft comforts of this or that Government House.

A year later, back in London at her parents' Bruton Street
house, the Duchess gave birth on April 21, 1926 to her first child,
a girl, Princess Elizabeth Alexandra Mary, who was to become
the Second Elizabeth, Sovereign Queen. It was a joyful event for
the Yorks, and a specially glad one for King George, for this was
the first grandchild in the male line. But neither the Press nor the
public, nor indeed the Royal Family, foresaw the baby as a
future Queen. Expectation was that as time went by she would
move further back rather than forward in the line of succession
to the Crown. Her grandfather was firmly on the Throne and in
the fullness of time his heir, the loved Prince of Wales, would
reign in his place; naturally it was assumed that he would marry
and have a family; and it would be they, not any *second* son's
children, who would be foremost in the succession order. So the
birth of Princess Elizabeth aroused friendly general interest, but
no great fuss. In any case, the General Strike a fortnight later
swept babies and almost everything else from the newspaper
pages.

In 1927 the parents rather reluctantly left their eight-month-
old daughter for a long spell in order to carry out a first and
formidable exercise in important royal duty overseas, an official
world tour. This was a particularly daunting undertaking for
the Duke who, though he had gained some confidence as a

public figure, was still nervous and highly strung when on
parade. Australia and New Zealand were the main countries
visited, and His Royal Highness knew that specially critical eyes
were on him out there because he was following a dazzlingly
successful visit by the Prince of Wales a few years earlier. The
triumphs of that Prince Charming brother were still glowingly
remembered by the people who now watched a man who
seemed to them at first a dutiful, but disappointingly dissimilar,
second string.

He tackled with determination the messages he had to speak at ceremony after ceremony, but the words did not come easily. It was at those moments that the sight of the Duchess, sitting with head held high and a smile on her face, not only calmed the speaker and helped him along but also soothed and reassured those who listened. Then, as the weeks went by, because he had Elizabeth's backing and belief in him, he began noticeably to grow in stature and in performance. Even when Her Royal Highness caught a chill and for a day or two was not with him, her influence was still there, enabling him to become better with his words.

In the event, he always responded well to challenge and to hazard. And both he and his wife faced hazard enough during that tour when, travelling homewards in HMS *Renown*, there came the frightening experience of fire at sea. Whilst the battle-cruiser was sailing without escort across the Indian Ocean and a thousand miles from land, fire broke out in the boiler room and flames spread rapidly until they were only a few feet away from the main oil tanks. The ship, half full of smoke, was under threat of inferno and explosion. The Duke was a naval officer at once. He went down to the seat of the fire to help those who were directing the fire-fighting and bringing out the casualties. The Duchess, deliberately evincing no sign of alarm even when decks became hot and the order to leave ship was about to be given, carried on as though she hardly noticed the emergency. There was no panic around *her*. At length, to the relief of all, the blaze was put out just in time; and the Yorks that night, instead of sitting in an open boat far from any shore – which is what they had begun to expect – went thankfully to their beds.

The Captain of *Renown* said afterwards to the Duchess: 'Did you realise, ma'am, that at one time it was pretty bad?' 'Yes, I did,' she replied. 'Every hour someone came to tell me that there was nothing to worry about – so I knew there was real trouble.'

When they returned from that tour, which had lasted half a year, they were greeted enthusiastically by a Princess 'Lilibet' who had become 'quite a handful' and, aged fourteen months, had just cut her fourth tooth. And with her they went into a new home.

When they were first married, the Duke and Duchess had lived at the White Lodge in Richmond Park, a house with a considerable royal history and the place were Queen Mary had grown up (today it is the home of the Royal Ballet School). But it was a monstrous great place struggling out of an era of gaslighting; it was cold and isolated, inconveniently sited, costly to run and inescapably antique.

The old mansion was also the place where the Duke of York's brother, the Prince of Wales, had been born, but he, David, had not seen it for years. So when he toured the house whilst Bertie and Elizabeth were living there he was appalled to find how out-of-date and uncomfortable it was.

So now, in 1927, the Yorks moved into London and spent the next decade at Number 145 Piccadilly (a house demolished before the last war), living almost like any other upper-class family, in reasonable privacy with neither crowds nor sentries at the door. In 1931, George V also gave them, to their great pleasure, a home out of town with gardens round it: the Royal Lodge in Windsor Great Park.

The birth of the Duchess's second child, however, took place at her old home, Glamis. The baby was another daughter. Princess Margaret Rose (whom her parents wished to call Anne, but the name was vetoed by the old King) emerged on a night of thunder and howling gale: August 21, 1930. She was the first member of the Royal Family to be born in Scotland for well over three hundred years. And the baby Margaret was a great joy, born though she was into a Britain gripped by the great Industrial Depression and the Hunger Marches.

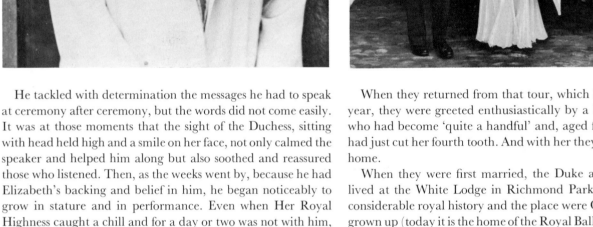

The two little girls were brought up together, educated at home by governesses and tutors working always under the careful guidance of their mother. It was their fate to live teenage years in wartime, conditioned by the restrictions and dangers of a besieged and embattled Britain.

But several years before the war's outbreak in 1939 – years when the dark shadows of the Dictators were only beginning to edge across Europe – a small cloud of a more intimate kind, a cloud that would later swell into a domestic and national cataclysm, nudged into the consciousness of the Royal Family. This shadow was not then in the public view, and even in the family circle was at first only a matter of frowns and eyebrow-raising, rather than immediate anxiety. It came from the figure who in the eyes of the world was the brightest of them all, that desirable David, the Prince of Wales and Heir to the Throne. Before long this cloud was to shake the Throne and profoundly change the life of the Yorks. In the end, it brought Elizabeth Bowes-Lyon to stardom.

Opposite, left *Another glimpse of the Duchess in 1929 style.*

Opposite right *The fashionable Duchess walks through old Brussels during 'British Week' at the International Exhibition in July 1935.*

Right *King George V in 1933 with the ladies of the family in front of the miniature Welsh Cottage, at Royal Lodge, Windsor.*

Below *In July 1931 at a Garden Party at Glamis Castle.*

CHAPTER 3

To be a Queen

DURING THE First World War the Prince of Wales, though still a very young man, had been in khaki and had served in France – courageous, eager for action, but not in fact allowed into the front line of battle. After the war was over, unsettled and uncertain like many of his generation, he had plunged vigorously into the cauldron of the variegated Society of the gay Twenties, hunting in very mixed company, party-going with feverish drive in a whirl of lively ladies and late nights. To the overseas world, in which the handsome young man travelled on whatever royal duties were handed out to him, and to the majority of the people of Britain, he was a sporting Beau Ideal, his superficial graces and good looks quite devastating. He was pictured and he was popular, smiling and sympathetic to the crowds he met. He sought to show an interest in social problems, miners' welfare, and foreign trade. To his brothers and sisters, certainly to the Duke of York and his Duchess, he was for the most part a relative of charm and kindness and good intentions. He was impressionable and affectionate. But also – and this was something which began the family's worry – he was increasingly in immature revolt against the Victorian code which still ruled in the house of George V.

The world of brother-in-law David and his new-found friends was not the Duchess of York's world. He and she met happily enough on royal duty and in the gatherings of the family. But then they went their different ways – he to his cocktail parties and she to a loved home and happy husband and children, the 'matchless blessing' which the elder brother of her husband was to envy publicly in his famous broadcast of farewell and handover in a sadly historic 1936.

Far from 'settling down' as his father prayed he would do, the Prince of Wales pursued his own bright way into the Thirties. His brother, Prince George who was the Duke of Kent (and nearest to David in spirit), married the beautiful Princess Marina of Greece in 1934; in the following year came the wedding of Prince Henry, Duke of Gloucester, to Lady Alice Montagu-Douglas-Scott, attractive daughter of a Scottish peer. But, for the eldest of the King's sons, it was affairs and adventures – and still no wife.

But he had met in London the woman who was to be the love of his life and for whom, later, he would quit the kingship and go into exile: Mrs Wallis Warfield Simpson. For most of the time that the association was growing, the public knew little or nothing of it. But in the Royal Family, though at first it was put to the back of their minds as something that would pass, more and more notice had reluctantly to be taken of David's consuming devotion to the smart lady from America. Mrs Simpson, already once divorced, was a well-groomed, well-read, clever and brightly entertaining New Socialite who talked with an ingratiating Baltimore drawl and who fascinated the Prince as no other woman before had done. She became his constant companion. With her and her friends, he drew more and more away from his family; he was in a new circle of gaiety. And the King, horrified but helpless, growled: 'The boy will ruin himself in twelve months after I'm gone.'

The state of King George V's health in the years after he had rallied from the illnesses of 1928 and 1931 was another secret kept from the public. The Duchess of York worried a good deal about the precarious hold on life which her father-in-law was just managing to keep. She made as much fuss of him as his nature, and her own, allowed. She had become much attached to him, knowing and sympathizing with his outlook more than his own children did. She discerned the kindness, simple honesty and the need to be liked, beneath the sometimes unprepossessing exterior. She personally knew the affection that was in the man – a quality which came through in that warm gravelly voice when

Opposite The royal couple with Princess Elizabeth and a corgi on the steps of 145 Piccadilly, their London home.

Right Edward VIII in 1936, the one year of his reign.

Left *In November 1936 King Edward VIII visited the mining district of South Wales. Here he is accompanied by Ernest Brown, then Minister of Labour (on his left) and Sir Kingsley Wood.*

Below *The Coronation of King George VI in Westminster Abbey on May 12, 1937.*

Opposite, top *There was also a Crown for Queen Elizabeth at the impressive ceremony in the Abbey.*

Opposite, bottom *The new Sovereign and Consort in the golden coach of the Coronation procession.*

he (the first monarch to use the wireless like this) made the Sovereign's Broadcasts each Christmas Day. He really *sounded* like the Father of His People, as indeed he was – an Emperor reigning unopposed for a quarter of a century, a period in which his relatives, the last Tsar and the last Kaiser, were harshly removed.

George V, first Sovereign of the House of Windsor, had no genius and no conceit. When he and Queen Mary celebrated their Silver Jubilee on May 6, 1935, driving through cheers in densely crowded streets, the welcome astonished and deeply

Left *The King and Queen on the balcony of Buckingham Palace with Princess Elizabeth, Princess Margaret and their attendants.*

Below *King George VI taking the salute at a distribution of medals to Overseas Contingents at Buckingham Palace two days after the Coronation. Behind him are Queen Elizabeth, Queen Mary, the Princesses Elizabeth and Margaret, and the Duchess of Gloucester.*

Opposite *Queen Elizabeth and Queen Mary with the two Princesses (a Guide and a Brownie) in the Quadrangle of Windsor Castle during a Girl Guide Rally at Windsor in 1938.*

moved him. At home in Buckingham Palace that night, before retiring early to bed as usual, whilst beacons burned and the nation still celebrated, he wrote in his diary: 'They must really like me.'

He had enjoyed his day. They all had. In another carriage in the royal procession to the Thanksgiving in St Paul's Cathedral rode the Duke and Duchess of York accompanied by their two girls, Princess Elizabeth (then nine years old) and Princess Margaret (four). It was a day specially to remain in the memory of the elder daughter who, forty-two years later, when she was a reigning Sovereign herself, rode through even greater waves of affection in the capital city on *her* Silver Jubilee and gave thanks in the same Cathedral. Young Lilibet she was in 1935, a child watching the bearded old man she called 'Grandpa England' join wholeheartedly with the congregation of four thousand

in the hymns and the prayers for all the blessings of life.

But even on that day the King was a sick man, his mind as racked by the war march of Germany's Brown Shirts as his body was by the conquering bronchitis. The Europe he knew was dying, and so was he. When the family gathered for that year's Christmas at Sandringham he was failing fast; he lasted only until January 20 – just before Hitler occupied the Rhineland. The news of the ending of the reign was broadcast in one of the most famous sentences of BBC bulletins: 'The King's life is moving peacefully to its close.'

Peace for him, but not for the world. Nor for the family he had left. A chapter had closed and in the chapter to come were events beyond forecasting – certainly so in the family at Number 145 Piccadilly where his brother's Accession made the Duke of York the immediate next in line to the Throne. Heir Presumptive was the title. But to the Duchess, as well as to her husband, it must have been believed and hoped that in fact Bertie was only the Heir *Provisional* – just a title and just for a few years probably.

To the Throne, then, came brother David, the Prince of Wales, now Edward VIII, forty-one years of age and still the Golden Boy, cynosure of great expectations and goodwill, focus of the ideals of a post-war generation still unwilling to believe that world war would come again. It was felt that kingship would now move with the times, and that the new king's way of life would rise to the serious responsibilities of his supreme office, though for him it would mean sacrifices and loss of loved informality. The loyalty and devotion of his own family was without question at his feet, and the people's hopes were upon him. Here was a vigorous monarch who would work for the welfare of his country and the peace of the world, at the same time bridging the gaps between eras and classes.

But it was not going to be like that. To be good-looking and emotive, full of good intentions and boyish enthusiasms was not enough. You had to work at being a king. Before long it became

plain to members of the Royal Family, as it became at a very late stage to the public, that, although he began by making earnest attempts to tackle the tasks of Head of State, Edward VIII was not able to reconcile what had become a self-indulgent private life with the duties of a constitutional sovereign. As time went on, his failings told. Often impatient and unstable, too easily discouraged, resentful of criticism and increasingly inconsiderate of others, he was impulsive without being inspired and had more charm than talent.

This new monarch, in 1936, soon began to spend time on brassy parties and boating holidays rather than studying State documents and performing at public ceremonies. Loathing stuffiness, anxious as ever to rush his fences, reforming all too brusquely some of the protocol and outmoded patterns of his father's Court, he caused dismay and offence by thoughtless staff economies. Inescapable duties irked him. Understandably, the old Establishment began to campaign against his ways. He wasn't being a good king.

Most worrying of all to the family, however, was the attachment to Mrs Simpson, which became stronger as the months of 1936 went by. Far from putting her aside when the change from Heir to Monarch came upon him, the King's feelings towards her and his desire for her company became all-engrossing. He was obsessively in love. Hers was the company he sought, theirs together the future he contemplated, notwithstanding forbidding differences in their stations and circumstances. She went everywhere with him, cruising abroad and even staying at Sandringham and Balmoral, at first as guest but later appearing in the role of hostess, bright with the jewels that were his gifts.

It was shocking to the Duke and Duchess of York, straining to understand and forgive though they were. They were saddened by the change in David towards themselves: he had become so often irritable, morose and thoughtless, not only with servants but also with his relatives. They hardly ever saw him. Once so affectionate and close, he was now difficult to get hold of, even on the telephone. He would stay at Fort Belvedere, a castellated folly near Virginia Water on the edge of Windsor Great Park, which he had made his own favourite country house. There he flung himself into bush-clearance gardening, entertaining assorted friends with high informality, and enjoying long week-end parties. No longer was he the Uncle David who would pop in to see the two Princesses and their mother and father. The one person who absorbed him was Mrs Simpson (soon to divorce Husband Number Two). The King was determined to make her his wife, whatever the cost, even if it meant giving up the Crown. Personally, he wanted her beside him on the Throne.

But the lady, a divorcee, could not be accepted by Britain or the Commonwealth as Queen or as the wife of a reigning King. A constitutional crisis developed and deepened, jarring many hopes and sympathies – for a desire for the King's happiness was widespread. It became clear that *his* desire was going to mean nothing less than renunciation of his whole office. Winston Churchill, royalist and romantic, dismayed at the thought of thrusting out a Monarch, and for once misjudging the feelings of Parliament and people, tried for a time to rally support for some sort of compromise or temporary move to delay a fateful departure. But the instinct of the majority of the public, an innate steadiness in the British nation, the decisions of Dominion and Home ministers against such things as morganatic marriages – all were against Edward VIII. He had to go.

The abdication was in fact virtually settled before most people in Britain were aware of the crisis. For although through many weeks and months the newspapers and magazines of half the world had been featuring and picturing the romance of the British King and Wallis Simpson, the Press and the BBC at home had hardly mentioned it.

Only on December 1 did the whole sensational story break in Britain's newspapers. Nine days later Edward VIII abdicated and, within hours, he left his native land. His had been a short-lived encounter with destiny. In his few months of monarchy he had become out of touch with his subjects, had failed to understand that his conduct had killed his charisma. Almost to the last, he could not credit how absolute his end would be. He reigned for less than a year and was never crowned. When he had gone, as Duke of Windsor he married Mrs Simpson in due course, a quiet wedding in France in June, 1937. His wife was styled Duchess, but never Her Royal Highness (he bitterly resented this as a slight and a denial of right); and there followed for the two of them thirty-five years of personal happiness together. But they were criticised, gradually almost forgotten, no doubt to be pitied. The Duke was to survive for nearly twenty years the brother who now, against all expectations and wishes, succeeded him as the 'Reluctant King'.

To say that the Abdication Crisis of 1936 was a shock for the Duke and Duchess of York is a monumental understatement. They had known about Mrs Simpson, met her briefly, found her alien to their way of life. The Duchess, like stately Queen Mary, was upset, but it was not her way to contemplate unpleasant possibilities. She and her husband had not tried to influence the new King over the lady of his choice any more than they had over his irresponsibility as Head of State. They had affection and sympathy for him, but he had cut himself off from them and

Opposite *Glamis Castle, owned by the Strathmores since 1372.*

Below *In July 1937 Queen Elizabeth, as Colonel-in-Chief, visited the armoured section of the Queen's Bays at Aldershot.*

Left *Through the centuries Glamis has been visited and lived in by many members of the Scottish and British Royal Families. Princess Margaret was born here. The illustration shows the Queen Mother's sitting-room, still used by her when she visits.*

Left, bottom *Of all the rooms at Glamis perhaps the Drawing Room, or Great Hall, is the most magnificent. Particularly interesting is the fireplace shown here, measuring thirteen-and-a-half feet in width and reaching to the spring of the ornate plasterwork ceiling, created in 1621. The vast canvas is of the third Earl with his sons.*

Right *Seated with her corgis outside her coastal Castle of Mey, in the northernmost part of the Scottish mainlaid.*

Below *During a visit to Caithness in the early months of her widowhood, Queen Elizabeth was told there was a possibility that old Barrogill Castle would be demolished. She decided there and then to buy it for her own use. Once the castle was restored she gave it the ancient name of the Castle of Mey, and it is to this retreat that she goes whenever she can. Here an informal Mey basks in the warm August sunshine, when Her Majesty was in residence.*

Opposite *Pink-washed, the Royal Lodge is set in the south-east corner of Windsor Great Park. From its derelict condition of 1931 it was transformed into 'home' for the Yorks.*

Below *In Paris, July 1938, Queen Elizabeth's clothes were immensely admired. Here she is seen at a Garden Party in the grounds of the Bagatelle Palace, the Bois de Boulogne.*

Early in 1947 the Royal Family toured South Africa. Here they arrive at a Garden Party given by the Governor-General at Westbroke, Rondebosch.

Queen Consort and an Empress at the age of thirty-six. Gone was the cosy house in Piccadilly: her home was the vast headquarters of the Monarchy, Buckingham Palace with its six hundred rooms, now housing its third reigning Sovereign within the space of twelve months. The change for her was difficult; the change for her husband and for the institution of the Crown was dramatic and could have been dangerous. An extrovert monarch, whom all the world knew, had quit and was being succeeded by a shy monarch who shunned publicity. Diligent and brave, but never physically robust, the new King had been a pale 'also ran' to the mercurial David, who had once shone so brightly that his departure might have been an irreparable disaster. The Abdication might have wrecked the British Monarchy. But that proved to be far from the case, and the long view of history may well be that the change *saved* the Monarchy. For an awkward iconoclast was replaced on the Throne by a brother who was a gentle and sensible progressive, a man whose transparent goodness became a loved national asset. Under George VI the Crown became more stable and more respected than ever.

How did the hesitant Bertie manage this miracle? The answer is that he did not – not by himself. The achievement was as much to the credit of the new Queen Consort as to him. She was an incomparable support. True, the sheer occupation of high office brought out the new Sovereign's best qualities; he grew in stature, presently gaining a confidence unknown before. He was demonstrably in control, making decisions that were wisely his own and quietly developing his dutiful qualities to the nation's advantage. He exercised regal authority, firmly, because that was now his duty. There was no *folie de grandeur* in him. He was a rock of good sense.

Nevertheless, no monarch has ever stood less alone than George VI, none has ever been endowed with so wonderful a partner. *Of course* he was thankfully dependant on the capabilities of the Queen with whom he would talk over his problems – how could he *not* take the help of the splendid wife who loved him and lived at his side! But that did not make him a weak king. It was simply that the character of Queen Elizabeth, the example of calm devotion, loyalty, and family unity which she presented to the world, as well as to him, did much to steady and strengthen the Throne. The manner in which she underpinned the new monarch's work of reconstruction after the damage of 1936 was invaluable. It might well have been impossible for George VI to have tackled kingship at all without that valiant wife. As it was, her cheerfulness and confidence, her reassuring influence when he was pessimistic and irascible, her belief in him which made him gradually more sure of himself, inspired him through all the years of their partnership. It enabled a good king to become a great one.

The new Queen at once began, resolutely and without any fear, to bring talent and commonsense to bear on *her* duties. The toqued, unbending figure of Queen Mary was in the background to support the regime, but none save the Consort could

never consulted his brother on what he intended to do. For a long time, the Duchess could hardly believe that the crisis would end in utter renunciation by him. Only in the last frenetic days, in consternation not helped by a bout of influenza, did she accept and bring her iron-willed calmness to bear upon the fact that she and the Duke were about to be precipitated into a life of kingship.

The Duchess had no illusions about the daunting task ahead. David, once so promising, so loved, was leaving his job, with all its exacting responsibilities, in the lap of a delicate, disconcerted and un-rehearsed brother. She knew that the brother, her husband, however unsought his Throne, would not shrink or spare himself in what were sure to be years of toil and peril ahead. It must have been her fear, even then, that the task would shorten her husband's life. She knew also that she was herself about to become a leading figure on the nation's stage – and she rose magnificently to her role.

Albert, Duke of York, became King George VI on December 11, 1936, three days before his forty-first birthday. His wife, the Elizabeth Bowes-Lyon of only a dozen years before, was now

Opposite, top *Queen Elizabeth on the balcony of the Home Office on Armistice Day, 1938. With her are the Duchess of Kent, Princess Helena Victoria and Queen Mary.*

Opposite, bottom *King George VI making a radio broadcast from the Governor's house in Winnipeg, Manitoba, on Empire Day 1939, during the Royal Tour of Canada.*

stand beside the King and run his house. And what a mansion she had moved into! Buckingham Palace was a great rambling world of its own. It had been an echoing mausoleum in Victoria's widowhood years, civilised in some degree by Edward VII, enriched in antique furnishing at least by Queen Mary, but it had remained a vastly complicated domain with stiff hierarchies Downstairs as well as Upstairs. The staff was numbered in hundreds: chefs and footmen, grooms and porters, specialists all in high or low degree, from Master of the Household and Steward and Housekeeper to maids and apprentices serving such personages as the Page of the Back Stairs and the Chief Yeoman of the Glass and China Pantry.

The First Lady faced them all with understanding and application. Soon she was sorting them out and setting the departments about their business. It did not take her long to make the private apartments homely as they had never been. Comfortable furniture was moved in from 145 Piccadilly; warm family character clothed the rooms as modern books, gramophone records, bright pictures, easy chairs and vases of massed flowers arrived.

It was soon after this time, when prime responsibilities and many public appearances were being undertaken, that Her Majesty was noticed, especially by the fashion-conscious, to be presenting not only a more mature, but also a markedly attractive figure in her manner of dressing. The eye-catching hats and brightly tasteful gowns appeared, the light furs and the pearl necklaces and the varieties of pastel colours in her ensembles. Sophisticated hairstyles replaced the fringe. The beautifully dressed Queen, to be an admired part of the British scene for a long time to come, was beginning to emerge.

After the Abdication trauma, the ordeal of the Crowning ceremony itself came upon this Sovereign and Consort more

quickly than is usual at the beginning of a reign. Normally, a Coronation takes place a year or more after Accession. But for them it was only five months later, for they adhered to the date that had been fixed for the brother who never reached it. Queen Elizabeth took a personal hand in much of the Coronation preparation. She attended planning conferences, studied the details, sent the invitations, went to rehearsals, and helped, together with Mr Logue, in the schooling of the King in the ordained responses he would be required to make in Westminster Abbey.

The ancient rite took place in all its pageantry on May 12, 1937 in a London thronged with cheering people. On this occasion the service in the Abbey *was* broadcast on the radio, but no such thing as a television camera was allowed in. There was, however, much filming in the streets outside, and, in the first-ever 'live' television outside broadcast, moving-pictures were transmitted directly to viewers by the BBC, whose public high-definition TV service, the first in the world, had started six months before.

Inside the Abbey, the whole Royal Family were assembled – from Queen Mary, now Queen Dowager, to her grandchildren, the two Princesses. Margaret was only six at the time, and had a struggle to keep awake as she watched the long ceremony from the Royal Gallery. It was the Crowning of both the girls' parents, for the Queen as well as the King. Things went happily and smoothly for Her Majesty when her turn came to kneel, and be blessed and annointed beneath a canopy held aloft by four duchesses.

But for the King, already keyed-up and nervously anticipating every detail, the service produced more than one contretemps. The Dean at one point tried to put a white surplice on His Majesty inside-out, and had to be corrected; at the altar, the

Archbishop, holding up the Form of Service for the King to read, accidentally covered with his thumb the very words of the Oath which it was the Monarch's duty to speak; the Lord Great Chamberlain fumbled so much over buckling-on the Sovereign's vestments that the King had to fix the sword-belt himself; there was clerical uncertainty and much twisting-about before they got St Edward's Crown, weighing seven pounds, the right way round on the royal brow; and the King was made to stumble and nearly fall down when a bishop trod on his robe and had to be told sharply by the Monarch to get off.

However, in spite of all those incidents, George VI was entirely in command. Queen Elizabeth watched him with anxiety and loving pride. She herself sailed through the whole day with smiling confidence.

They were both now deep in public engagements and the cares of State. Deep too in the mounting anxieties of an ominous international situation. Europe lay under totalitarian threat from the conquering Nazis, now annexing territories in a drift to war, which was only briefly stayed by Neville Chamberlain's return from Germany waving a piece of paper from Hitler. He had bought but little time by the Munich surrender: 1938 was a dolorous year.

It was also the year of personal sadness for the Queen, for Lady Strathmore, the gifted mother who had been in poor health for some time, died in July. Family mourning for the Countess caused postponement of the State Visit to France, but in the autumn the King and Queen did go to Paris and were effervescently acclaimed.

Their return from France was at the same time that, in expectation of war, trenches were being dug in the London parks and gasmasks were being issued – to Palace people like everybody else. The Fleet was mobilized, the evacuation of children from the cities ordered. At the end of September the King should have gone to Clydebank to launch the world's largest liner which was to bear his wife's name, but the crisis kept him in London and the Queen travelled north to perform the ceremony in his stead.

On the following day, September 28, the Chamberlain surrender to Hitler – for so it proved – staved off the outbreak of war. But the Munich 'Agreement' was an appeasement which put off the inevitable for a bare twelve months only.

But during that summer – on advice, for it was time for Britain to be strengthening friendships – a long-planned royal visit to Canada and the United States was undertaken, despite the gravity of the international situation. The King and Queen crossed the Atlantic in May and then carried out the full North American programme as planned. Happening though it was so clearly on the eve of war, the tour was a memorable success, most certainly for the Queen. She made an impression both as a charming person and a convincing representative of her country. She helped to rebuild Anglo-US understanding at a time of strain, for many Americans at that time were, to say the least of it, alarmingly neutral and isolationist in their attitude to the openly venomous Hitler and his odious jackal Mussolini, and apparently indifferent also to the prospect of a conflict to save Europe.

In her contacts and conversations the Queen evidently did something more besides. Whatever her private views may have been over recent events in the Royal Family, she did a great deal to dispel certain misapprehensions on the other side of the Atlantic, where it was believed by some that Britain was a hotbed of anti-American sentiment and that the real reason for Edward VIII's 'dismissal' was the Duchess of Windsor's nationality.

Queen Elizabeth looked beautiful on that trip, crinolines, tiaras and all. Just what a Queen ought to look like, they thought in the many cities, towns and villages visited during the long journeys across a continent. Day after day she and the King left the royal train and, to the consternation of the security men, plunged into the crowds to make sensational 'walk-abouts' (this was many years before the Australian word was taken up and overworked by today's journalists to describe the *second* Elizabeth's excursions). The Canadian Province of Québec specially loved the visitors, and applauded their polished French accents. The Press photographers discovered the Queen's news-picture sense: she seemed always to pause naturally just where they hoped she would, enabling them to get good shots with the light right and the now-famous smile shining. Quite as remarkable as the welcomes in the Canadian cities were the cheers which deafened them in small communities – Moose Jaw, Medicine Hat, Sioux Lookout and Kicking Horse Pass.

In the Royal Train they slowly crossed the plains and rumbled through the Rockies. There were innumerable halts, and at the tracksides in even the tiniest of places, knots of men, women and children, many of them on horseback, would be

gathered, to cheer and to wave and then to chatter as the two royal tourists stepped down to mix amongst them for a while. Nor were the welcomes confined to the scheduled stops. In lonely places over thousands of miles, people drove or rode across rough country to stand beside the line and wait for hours, simply to see the train go by. Queen Elizabeth gave instructions that the King and she must be told whenever the engine driver observed a collection of people by the side of the line ahead, so that they could be waving-back at the window, to see and be seen, as the train went slowly along.

At one time, very late in the night, word came back on the telephone from the driver's cab that the train would be passing an unusually large country group a few miles ahead, and that people had trekked great distances to be there. The Queen got up, wrapped a warm dressing-gown round her, did her hair and put one of her best tiaras on, and was to be seen, well-lit on the royal coach's observation-platform as the train went at a snail's pace through the crowd. (She was never one to disappoint a gathering. I remember her, one sweltering African morning during another tour, dressing-up in jewels and full evening gown at 10 a.m. to appear at a Zulu assembly – 'because that is how they'd expect me to look, and they'd know it was me.')

When the King and Queen crossed the border into the USA on that 1939 tour they were the first reigning Sovereign and

Consort to set foot on American soil. President Roosevelt and his wife were their hosts; and again they were greeted by great crowds. In the capital, a newspaper headline announced: 'The British re-take Washington.' In New York, thousands of people at the World's Fair sang 'Land of Hope and Glory' and shouted 'Attaboy, Queen!' Columnists nominated her Woman of the Year. As Hitler loomed on the other side of the Atlantic, it was certainly this royal lady who played a leading part in turning America's tide of affection back to Britain.

Arriving back in the United Kingdom at the end of it all, the travellers were met by a display of public affection beyond anything expected. For the reports of their transatlantic triumph had come flooding ahead of them, showing that the visit had been a perfect winner, the antithesis of the perfunctory plod by a bashful couple through lukewarm prairies which some critics had predicted. Politicians and people realised afresh what they had acquired: a King and Queen of captivating appeal and new-found professional assurance. On the brink of world tragedy though we were – and indeed partly *because* we were – men and women turned loyally and gratefully to this royal couple who were becoming a focus of national identity and purpose. Established and respected in their own right now, they were to win the further pride of a nation in combat during the five years to come.

Opposite *When the* Empress of Britain *docked at Southampton, bringing Their Majesties home from their visit to Canada and the United States, the two Princesses boarded the liner to greet their parents. Here two small page boys present giant pandas to the Princesses on behalf of the crew.*

Right *The King and Queen inspect a child's book during a visit to the Elementary School section of the Royal Agricultural Society's Centenary Show in Windsor Great Park in July 1939.*

CHAPTER 4

The Years of War

THE CLOUDS of conflict darkened fearfully over Europe in that summer of 1939, and the German forces' invasion of Poland on the first day of September faced Britain with a resort to arms no longer avoidable. National mobilisation was declared at once, and the Second World War began on September 3.

During the ensuing years of peril and unprecedented suffering King George and Queen Elizabeth became an historic team, a Sovereign partnership standing fast through thick and thin. Their personal resolution was an acknowledged inspiration. In hours of crisis and at moments of thanksgiving for victories, crowds would make their way to Buckingham Palace to stand at the railings and call for the two who had stayed on at the centre of it all, leaders and representatives of a nation, symbolizing with courage and anguish the challenge to freedom. They wanted to see their Royals, to share the dark days and then the gleams of liberation with the two Palace people who themselves were sharing the war's dangers and setting examples of steadfastness and valour.

Through those years the King and Queen accepted like everybody else the raids and the rationing and the harrowing experiences which at times made life on the Home Front as perilous as on battlegrounds overseas. The Norfolk country house, Sandringham, was closed, its golf course ploughed up for food-growing. Whilst the King and Queen remained in London, the two Princesses were sent off to live at Windsor where there was a strong shelter to sleep in when the air attacks came. Occasionally the family managed a visit to Scotland or to the Sandringham farmlands. In Buckingham Palace, a new austerity prevailed. When in the middle of the war Mrs Eleanor Roosevelt stayed there, she was astonished at the cold and damp which was allowed to creep into the enormous place ('and just one little bar of electric fire in the room'), at the few inches of bath water, and at the canteen food which was served on the royal plates.

Earlier, the Queen's house had been a sanctuary for royal refugees. As the German armies overran Europe and London became a rallying point for men and women who had emerged from the onslaught to continue in exile to fight for freedom, the hospitality of the Palace was given to Heads of State from other countries who, evading Nazi drives to capture them, arrived in Britain as escapees. One of those monarchs was the ageing Queen Wilhelmina of The Netherlands who, when she arrived and was received by Queen Elizabeth, was wearing a tin hat and had only the clothes she stood up in. Another arrival was

Opposite The King and Queen viewing the damage at the cinema attached to Madame Tussaud's, bombed in September 1940.

Norway's tall King Haakon who, like many guests-of-war at this time, was concerned at the British Royal Family's disregard of danger and the apparent lack of security around them. This greatly worried the visitors because of their own experiences of being hunted by German troops and the knowledge that there existed, now that Britain itself was under threat of invasion, an enemy plan to capture the King and Queen and hold them hostage for the subservience of their people to Nazi conquerors.

It was only when pressure had been put on Their Majesties to make them realise that their personal safety was a matter of importance, that an effective two-room concrete and gas-proof shelter was constructed under the Palace, and even later that they considered the idea of a bullet-proof car in reserve to take them from London to the country if there were imminent threat of field-grey storm-troopers dropping on to their home. Doing an inelegant bolt when alarms sounded was not the habit of Queen Elizabeth: after urgent warning of air-raid sirens, when ladies-in-waiting and servants were prudently descending to shelter, she was more likely to be discovered in unhurried progress through upstairs apartments gathering up pet dogs and reading matter in case she had to spend a subterranean hour during the bombing. There was no question in her mind of leaving London. 'We stay put with our people' was the order of the day. Indeed, determined to go down fighting and not run if invasion came – as in 1940 it seemed likely to do – the King and Queen added shooting practice to gasmask drill, Her Majesty being given instruction in firing revolvers.

More than once, when things looked black for beleaguered Britain, it was suggested that the Queen at any rate, taking the two Princesses, should leave the country for the safety of Canada. The Queen's reply was: 'The Princesses cannot go without me. I cannot go without the King. The King will never go.' And that was that.

Their Majesties did remain in London during the worst of the Blitzes. The Palace itself was hit by bombs, flying bombs and rockets nine times, and the King and Queen had narrow escapes from death – experiences disclosed, and not by them, only after the war was over. One morning in 1940 they were working on some papers with a Household official in a sitting room overlooking the quadrangle when without warning the roar of an approaching aircraft was heard and, looking out, they saw a plane coming out of low cloud and streaking straight down the line of The Mall towards them and flying not far above the treetops. All in seconds, they saw bombs fall and heard the missiles' screams. The quadrangle outside their windows exploded just as the King was pulling his wife to the floor, where they lay with debris falling round them. Other crashes followed

Below *Their Majesties, wearing their gasmask haversacks, leave St Paul's Cathedral on the Day of National Prayer in October 1939. The Lord Mayor of London is behind the king.*

Bottom *A smile from the Queen for the residents of Kennington, during a visit to the Duchy of Cornwall Estate in London in the early months of the war.*

Opposite, left *Mr Churchill with the King and Queen on the steps of Number 10 Downing Street, October 1941.*

Opposite, right *The King and Queen with Princesses Elizabeth and Margaret during a week-end at Windsor.*

as the Luftwaffe's daylight raider dropped a stick of bombs right across the Palace and screamed away. The next thing that was heard as the King and Queen got to their feet was the sound of water coming through shattered windows: columns of spray were shooting up in the quadrangle as mains burst and underground sewers were breached. Deep and noisome craters were to be seen through the smoke.

In all the Palace bombings, casualties were light but much damage was done. (The Queen Mother thinks there is an unexploded bomb somewhere in the garden to this day.) Until temporary repairs could be made, baths and buckets stood in State Rooms and grand corridors to catch the rainwater coming in through shattered roofs. The Palace Chapel was completely destroyed by a direct hit. Pictures were in danger from fire and flood. The Queen was concerned to save, not so much their own belongings and furniture, as national treasures in London and Windsor: as many things as possible were removed to safety. 'We were never quite sure what was going to disappear in the next raid,' Her Majesty confessed later. 'We got Cecil Beaton to take photographs of the Palace damage, as a matter of historical record. And because it was possible, we thought, that even Windsor Castle might be at any rate partially destroyed, John Piper was asked to do a whole series of drawings of the Castle, to preserve its appearance for posterity.' (These pictures, full of the feeling of Royal Windsor and its stormy history, are today in the Lancaster Room of the Queen Mother's London home, Clarence House, where she recently said: 'Nothing terrible happened to Windsor, and now we have both the Pipers and the Castle.')

Her Majesty has most vivid recollections of the war years. Nobody remembers *her* showing fear, but she was aware enough of the dangers everybody risked. She saw that her personal affairs were in order, and wrote letters to her daughters and left them, sealed, in a place of safety, to be delivered only if she and the King became victims of enemy attack. She visited many bereft families; she lived with scenes of destruction when the raids were on. After her own home had been damaged she confessed: 'I'm almost comforted that we've been hit. It makes me feel I can look the blitzed East End in the face. They are so brave. The Cockney is a very good fighter.' And off to Hackney she went.

During the intensive bombing of London in 1940 and the devastation caused by the 'doodlebugs' and rockets later in the war, the King and Queen were often the first people from outside the immediate neighbourhood to go to an area of devastation. Picking their way through the smoking rubble of buildings and the fountains from punctured fire hoses, whilst the living and the dead were being brought from beneath collapsed houses, they would give what comfort they could to stricken people. The sight of them moving through newly ravaged streets, where as often as not there were unexploded land-mines around them, was a constant occurrence in many harrowing situations. Such was the prevailing spirit of 'London can take it!' that men and women stood beside the ambulances and the wreckage of their homes cheering, offering mugs of black-brewed tea, and producing from heaven knows where a few Union Jacks to wave to the gaunt figure in uniform and the resolute wife beside him. There were days when Chief

Constables wept at the sights of destruction as they crunched along in royal escort.

The Queen, though intensely moved, was by her training able to hold back the outward signs of grief. It was her business to talk, to comfort, to help gently with rescue and relief, even if sometimes it meant only holding a crying baby for a while, and whenever possible to send some of her own clothing through an agency to families whose possessions had been sent up in flames.

Not only the blitzed areas of London were visited, not only the bomb-shocked streets. The King and Queen went to hospitals, air-raid shelters, gun sites and searchlight batteries, fire stations and first-aid posts, Defence command centres and the secret headquarters of Government Ministries.

They travelled half a million miles in the Royal Train, sleeping in sidings where railway Home Guards stood watch against any possible attention by saboteurs or fifth column. Hull, Portsmouth, Bath, Swansea, Coventry – people of almost every bombed city saw them in their midst. Factories and airfields, camps and army training areas were visited; the Queen's gift for drawing people out, the sympathetic questioning which made men talk to her readily about their own lives, was the point of hundreds of stories. A United States sergeant burst into homespun tribute, as the royal visitor left the base where he had just met her. 'That was a real swell Queen!' he told his buddies. 'Talked to me like she was Mom. She was sure interested in every darn thing, even my old man's stomach ulcer.' She left a trail of brightness and laughter even in the war years.

Those who were close to her said that the only times they saw a flicker of fear and nervousness was when the King went overseas to see his troops in North Africa and Europe. She was restless until she had news that he had landed safely at his destination; she relaxed again only when he was back with her and they were at work together. They rarely had a day off.

Princess Elizabeth and Princess Margaret spent the Hitler Years out of the limelight. But in 1942, when she was sixteen,

By August 1941 Sandringham Park had been ploughed up and planted out for war-time food production. Whenever they could, the Royal Family personally inspected their growing crops.

Princess Elizabeth registered for National Service like any other young woman (after putting on her Girl Guide uniform to go the Labour Exchange). Two years later, having persuaded her parents to allow her to join a uniformed corps and serve on the Home Front, she entered the Auxiliary Territorial Service and in due course became a Junior Officer in a transport section, officially qualified 'to drive and maintain all classes of military vehicles'. (Her daughter's enthusiasm was reflected at the time, when the Queen remarked: 'We had sparking plugs all last night at dinner.')

In May, 1945 peace came with the surrender of Germany, and on Victory-in-Europe Day, Buckingham Palace was, as ever, the magnet for huge crowds: they stood cheering and singing until after midnight on the day hostilities ended, time after time demanding an appearance on the Palace balcony of the King and Queen, the Princesses, and the wartime Prime Minister, Winston Churchill.

At that time Japan had still to be defeated, but there was great thankfulness that the main menace, Hitler's Germany, had been overcome by the armed forces of the Allies. And on the VE Day, two of the figures grouped on the Palace balcony were still in Forces' uniform: the King as a naval officer and Princess Elizabeth (aged nineteen then) as an officer of the full-time ATS. Princess Margaret, still only fourteen, was not old enough to be in uniformed war service.

Characteristically, the King and Queen had thought for their daughters' enjoyment in the hours of public jubilation. That evening they allowed the two Princesses, in the care of a party of young Guards officers, to join the crowds in Whitehall and in the Mall as – in the forgotten luxury of street lights – they danced and shouted their joy at the ending of European war. 'Poor darlings,' the King wrote in his diary, 'they have never had any fun yet.'

There was peace then, but still privation. The weeks after the war ended gave us time to realise our shortages – and family anxieties. The Queen was worried over her husband's obvious tiredness. She knew better than anyone how much the tragedies of the five years – his own brother, the Duke of Kent, had been killed in an air crash whilst on active service in 1942 – had taken their toll of a man far from shockproof.

It was a measure of the King's sensitiveness to setbacks and the misfortunes of others that he was deeply grieved by what he felt was the 'ungrateful rejection' of his friend Churchill in the July General Election, as a result of which the man who had led Britain to victory and the world out of a jackboot thrall was dismissed by demobilized voters craving a Brave New World. The world which George VI was now concerned with was the world of the Labour Party and Mr Attlee, the atomic bomb and Mr Truman. Domestic life in Britain continued to be depressingly restricted. Unrelieved rationing, food queues, spending cuts and successive economic crises meant a hangover of drabness on the country.

The drabness was something Queen Elizabeth found specially hard to bear. It was in her nature to long, possibly more than most people did, for a return to colour and brightness in life. She had entered the war as a young married woman, had stood up cheerfully to the dangers and also the sheer ugliness of the years in which discomfort and austerity were virtues, and now, in her mid-forties, she was required to respect with more patience than was natural the slow pace at which gracious things returned to a weary world.

Above *Princess Elizabeth with her parents on her eighteenth birthday. The date was April 21, 1944.*

Left *Smiles all around as the King and Queen mingle with the people of the East End of London in Victory Year, 1945.*

CHAPTER 5

Peace–and Tragedy

THE ENDING of hostilities made it possible, at any rate, for the King and Queen quietly to demobilize themselves and ease back into regular peacetime occasions requiring their presence and patronage. Normal routines of State and public appearance were gradually resumed – something welcome and refreshing to the Queen, who, besides having become the complete professional herself in the business of being Royal, knew that the King with her great help had come to full stature and assurance.

And the family were able to be together again. What was more – as her mother was the first to discern – romance was in the air for Princess Elizabeth, the Heir to the Throne. She was in love with a fair-haired and noticeably good-looking young naval officer, Prince Philip of Greece, nephew of Lord Mountbatten, whom she had first met at Dartmouth Royal Naval College in 1939 when she was thirteen and he eighteen (the same age difference as that between the Queen and the King). Attraction was mutual; it increased as the two young

people met more and more frequently after the war, the high-speed arrivals of the Philip Mountbatten sports car at a side entrance to palace or castle becoming almost routine weekend phenomena.

An engagement might have been announced at Christmas 1946, but the King and Queen were about to go on a long tour through South Africa, taking the Princesses with them; they persuaded their elder daughter that no announcement should be made until that journey was over. For Elizabeth the tour meant four months away from Philip, and neither she nor he relished the prospect of separation. But Their Majesties felt that the break would give the young couple a situation in which they could fully know their own minds and be quite sure of their feelings for one another. So off went the King and Queen and the two girls, off from the most arctic British winter of modern times in HMS *Vanguard*, the latest (and last) battleship of the Royal Navy.

Opposite *Princess Elizabeth and Prince Philip, Duke of Edinburgh, at Buckingham Palace on their Wedding Day, November 20, 1947.*

Above *King George VI takes the salute as the mechanised column passes during the Victory Procession on June 8, 1946.*

Princess Elizabeth celebrated her twenty-first birthday during the tour – and came back 'quite sure' about Philip. *He* hadn't changed either; and soon after the travellers' return her betrothal to Lieut Mountbatten RN – now of British nationality – was made public. It was a popular announcement.

The wedding, its details joyfully organized by the bride's mother, took place on November 20, 1947. The Order of Service papers in Westminster Abbey still said that the Princess was marrying 'Lieutenant Philip Mountbatten', but in fact on the night before the wedding the King had conferred the title of Duke of Edinburgh on the man who was taking away his Lilibet.

In London streets on the wedding day large numbers of people, taking a day off work, packed the sidewalks and the windows of the processional route to cheer not only the bride and groom but the splashes of the old pre-war pageantry which the authorities had allowed to embellish the occasion. The cavalcades were a brief but heart-warming gleam in a world still dull and difficult and barely out of khaki. We had not seen the Household Cavalry in their full-dress splendour for almost a decade.

Less than six months later, on April 26, 1948, King George VI and Queen Elizabeth celebrated their Silver Wedding, another event publicly marked and publicly acclaimed during the royal drives to St Paul's Cathedral for a service of thanksgiving for twenty-five years of married happiness. The Queen was a picture in a silver-blue gown with a sweeping train. Characteristically, conscious of domestic hardships still gripping the nation,

Above The King and Queen, the Princesses and Lieutenant Philip Mountbatten arrive at Romsey Abbey on October 22, 1947. Princess Elizabeth and Princess Margaret were bridesmaids at the wedding of Lady Patricia Mountbatten, Earl Mountbatten's daughter, to Lord Brabourne. It was only one month before Princess Elizabeth's own marriage.

she spoke that day not only of her own joy in a loved home and family, but of others in her thoughts, people who could not at that time have such felicity. 'My heart goes out,' she said, 'to all who are living in uncongenial surroundings and who are longing for the time when they will have a home of their own.' Her words were heard and appreciated in many a crowded house in patched-up streets that were still gap-toothed from Hitler's bombs.

Another time of rejoicing in 1948 was November 14, the day on which Princess Elizabeth gave birth to her first child, a son, Charles Philip Arthur George, today's Prince of Wales, first of a new generation. The Queen was 'Grannie' for the first time, and very proud, particularly glad that the boy was to be called

Opposite A photograph of the Saloon, largest and handsomest room at Royal Lodge, Windsor – one of a number of photographs taken for this book by gracious permission of Her Majesty Queen Elizabeth The Queen Mother. On these walls hang a huge Brussels tapestry, a Windsor Park hunting scene, and (over the fireplace) a portrait of George IV by Sir Thomas Lawrence.

Opposite *From the Saloon at Royal Lodge, five French windows like this one lead to the broad terrace and magnificent views of the house's lawns and woodlands.*

Below *The spacious and comfortably furnished Octagon Room at Royal Lodge has the Queen Mother's desk in the corner where, at a turn of the head, she can see the path beside her loved rose garden.*

Above *View of the East Front of The Castle and the Sunken Garden.*

Left *View of the Sunken Garden from the East Front Rooms of the Castle.*

Charles, a name that glows in the Scottish history to which she has always been romantically and knowledgeably attached. Again, at the news of this birth, people gathered to sing and cheer in front of the Palace. At the other end of The Mall, the fountains in Trafalgar Square changed hue and the water turned blue 'for a boy'.

But shadow as well as sunshine came that year, for it was then that concern over the King's health began to cloud the family picture. The gravity of the situation was not at first known to the public, and indeed not fully to Princess Elizabeth in the months of her pregnancy, for her father had insisted that the extent of his suffering should be kept from her until after the birth of the baby. The fact was that, as a new life entered the family, the tide of the grandfather's life began to ebb. When Prince Charles was born, George VI lay ill under the same roof. The illness was serious. Abdication and Armageddon had taken their toll through the years, but the King's trouble was more than a legacy of war strain. The cramp in the legs of which His Majesty had been complaining was diagnosed, once the specialists were called in, as circulation trouble, hardening of the arteries and danger of gangrene. A public announcement, cancellation of engagements, and a period of complete rest indoors – all these had to follow – and once more a burden of anxiety lay upon the Queen. Inwardly distraught at this frightening misfortune to a husband who was only beginning his middle years, she maintained the outward calm and self-control which has been a mainstay of her make-up throughout her life. The Queen fulfilled on her own many of what would have been the Sovereign's outside engagements, at the same time making it her business to keep the King restfully and agreeably occupied whilst the medical treatment kept him indoors. Her serene presence and cheerfully considerate manner were a blessing to patient and doctors alike.

The King responded well to his treatment and was able to go to Sandringham and make his Christmas broadcast as usual. He was sufficiently improved to conduct an investiture at the Palace early in 1949, though he bestowed the accolades and insignia sitting down. But in March the specialists had to tell the Queen that the King's right leg was still obstructed, and that there would have to be an operation. This, a lumbar sympathectomy, was performed at once and was successful. But from then onwards the King was to moderate permanently his manner of life and work, abandoning all but the gentler duties. To say that he did so reluctantly is to put it mildly. To say that the Queen took on two people's work with shining resolution and infectious optimism is no overstatement. She was a pillar of both domestic duty and public life. Unhesitatingly she accepted what had to be. Nor was there a carefree existence for Princess Elizabeth in the early years of her married life; even whilst the young wife of a serving naval officer, she had to take leave of much private enjoyment in order to tackle a share of royal duties.

But her growing family was one of the chief joys of her own existence, as it was for her father in his declining years. Princess Elizabeth's second child, Anne, was born on August 15, 1950 –

Right, top *A pensive moment, during the Royal Family's visit to Edinburgh in July 1947.*

Right *The Royal Family attending a Garden Party at Port Elizabeth in February 1947, during the tour of South Africa.*

at Clarence House, which the Princess and the Duke of Edinburgh had at that time made their home. The King could not see enough of his lively grandchildren. Their visits to him were pure pleasure and a tonic.

He was able to play his part at the opening of the Festival of Britain, with its spectacular pavilions on the South Bank of the Thames, in the spring of 1951; but soon afterwards he became unwell again. It appeared to be influenza but proved to be catarrhal inflammation of the left lung. And in the autumn the patient faced with exemplary courage the ordeal of a major operation for the removal of a malignant growth. The 'lung resection' was carried out in a Palace room which had been turned into an operating theatre. There was the utmost concern for the Monarch's life; but slowly and bravely he came through. Doctors and nurses at the time spoke of the stamina and style with which the Queen, who hardly left her husband's bedside for a week, brought her loving and quietly confident influence to bear on the patient, and also on the medical team.

Little by little the King gained strength, and when Christmas came he was yet again able to make the usual journey to

Top *Quiet thanksgiving after the drive through cheering crowds. In 1948 King George VI and Queen Elizabeth had been married twenty-five years. The Silver Wedding Service was held in St Paul's Cathedral on April 26.*

Above *Two Queens, each with a distinctive style, go shopping in 1948 in King's Lynn, the Norfolk town close to Sandringham. Lynn townsfolk are quite accustomed to seeing the Royal Family in their midst.*

Opposite *Photographed on their Silver Wedding Anniversary with Princess Margaret as they pass along the Embankment on their return journey to the Palace after the Service of Thanksgiving in St Paul's.*

Sandringham. But this time there was no question of Christmas Day being an ordeal for him until the BBC's three o'clock Sovereign's Message was broadcast, when he could come away from the microphone with his tension gone. Each year until now he had insisted on making the broadcast 'live', hard though it was for him to do so, but now the loss of a lung had affected his breathing and accentuated the speech difficulty. So the 1951 Message had to be tackled in advance in a special way. During early December, in a series of 'takes' in his own room at Buckingham Palace, the speech was painstakingly pre-recorded by His Majesty bit by bit, phrase by phrase, until finally the tapes could be edited and joined by the BBC technicians into one short, but complete and coherent, address. And, on the day,

in the calm of his room in Norfolk, the King was able for once to listen to himself on the radio.

Millions received the broadcast with sympathy and a sense of sadness. The weariness in the voice, the battle that was evident in the frail man's slow and husky tones, and words of simple faith which he used as he counted his blessings, brought tears to the eyes and apprehension to the hearts of many who listened.

However, early in 1952, his family were cheered to notice that the King seemed to be improving a little in body as well as in spirit. He spoke optimistically of days to come. Overseas travel was out of the question, however, and it was Princess Elizabeth and her husband who set off in his stead to make what was to have been a five months' tour of Australia and New Zealand, by

way of Africa. On a bitterly cold day, January 31, the King went, with the Queen and Princess Margaret, to see his emissaries leave London by air. I shall never forget what was to prove the last sight of George VI. In the Heathrow Airport lounge the *au revoirs* had been said; more good-byes inside the aircraft and a last wave from Elizabeth and Philip before the door shut and the big airliner began to taxi slowly away. It went from sight to the distant end of the runway.

But the King did not move. Bareheaded, gaunt, he remained standing on the open windswept tarmac, reluctant to turn away. The Queen stayed beside him. He strained his eyes to watch not only the take-off but the steady climb of the royal Argonaut into the leaden sky. Only after the last speck of it was lost to view was

Above *A carefree afternoon on the moors in 1949.*

Right *Prince Charles gets his share of attention after the christening of Princess Anne on October 2, 1950.*

Opposite *The infant Prince Charles, who slept peacefully throughout his christening on December 15, 1948, is held by Queen Elizabeth in the Music Room of Buckingham Palace.*

he persuaded by the Queen to go inside to the warmth of the airport building.

It was the last farewell to his Lilibet, and perhaps he knew it. One week later he was dead and his daughter was back on that same spot at London Airport as reigning Queen.

The King had gone to Norfolk after seeing Elizabeth and Philip leave. He had a day or two of rest at his beloved Sandringham, and on February 5, which was Keepers' Day, he was out and about in fine weather, enjoying some rough shooting with the light gun he had begun to use. He spent a happy and contented evening in the house, retired to bed in good time – and during the night died peacefully in his sleep.

And so there passed away – at what hour nobody will ever know, for the King was found dead when his valet went into the bedroom with a cup of tea the next morning – a devoted and diligent Sovereign, a man who delighted in private family life but carried out public and constitutional duties to the utmost of his ability. Now he would struggle no more, this courageous, quiet man who might have seemed for a moment in 1936 a sad Sovereign Surrogate but who grew to become one of our best and best-loved kings. He lived only fifty-six years, and now his Queen was a widow at fifty-one.

Their elder daughter, at once no longer Princess but Sovereign Queen at the age of twenty-five, flew home from Africa in the black clothes of mourning. She had been four

Above *This unique photograph gives Birkhall a jewel-like appearance against a majestic Scottish backcloth. Birkhall is Her Majesty's Aberdeenshire home.*

Right *The gardens at Birkhall are largely the creation of Queen Elizabeth. Here is a view of the side entrance.*

Opposite, top *The King broadcasting to the world on May 3, 1951, that the Festival of Britain was open. He is speaking from the portico of St Paul's Cathedral where a Service of Dedication had just been held.*

Opposite, bottom *Queen Elizabeth chats with Winston Churchill after the marriage of the then Marquess of Blandford and Miss Susan Hornby.*

Left *The Log Cabin is a new joy for the Queen Mother during her Highland holidays, a picnic rendezvous used almost daily. This is her view from the side balcony, across the water to the woods of the North bank.*

Below *This Cabin, an Eightieth Birthday gift to Queen Elizabeth from her family and friends, is in a delightful setting beside the River Dee on the Balmoral estates. It looks downstream over Her Majesty's favourite fishing pool – the Polveir.*

thousand miles away in Kenya, her world tour scarcely begun, when the news of her father's death reached her on February 6, 1952. In fact she succeeded to the Throne at night, whilst watching big game in a tree-house in the Aberdare Forest, almost on the Equator. Although for two years she had known that her father's death might come at any time, the shock of losing this loved parent was grievous.

But the blow fell heaviest upon her mother Queen Elizabeth, 'that most valiant woman', as Churchill called her in his tribute at the time. For she had been constantly and with the utmost faith and devotion at her husband's side in days of joy and sorrow, peace and war, for almost three decades. She bore the premature ending of her cherished partner's life with iron control and a fortitude all the more exemplary because it meant, in her case, the loss not only of a husband but also of a position and a whole pattern of life. At a stroke, the posts and prerogatives of Queen Consort were gone and she was thrust into a loneliness which not even a family's love could assuage. Suddenly, she was no longer the Power Beside the Throne; she was mistress of the Palace no more. Queen Elizabeth's world perforce collapsed. Her first daughter was First Lady now, walking the path of service for which her mother with gentle wisdom had trained her.

Above *January 1952. The Royal Family leaving Drury Lane Theatre on the eve of the departure of Princess Elizabeth and the Duke of Edinburgh for what should have been a tour of Kenya, Ceylon, Australia and New Zealand. In fact they had reached only Kenya when the King died a week later.*

Right *Three Queens – Queen Elizabeth II, Queen Mary and Queen Elizabeth The Queen Mother – in mourning for King George VI.*

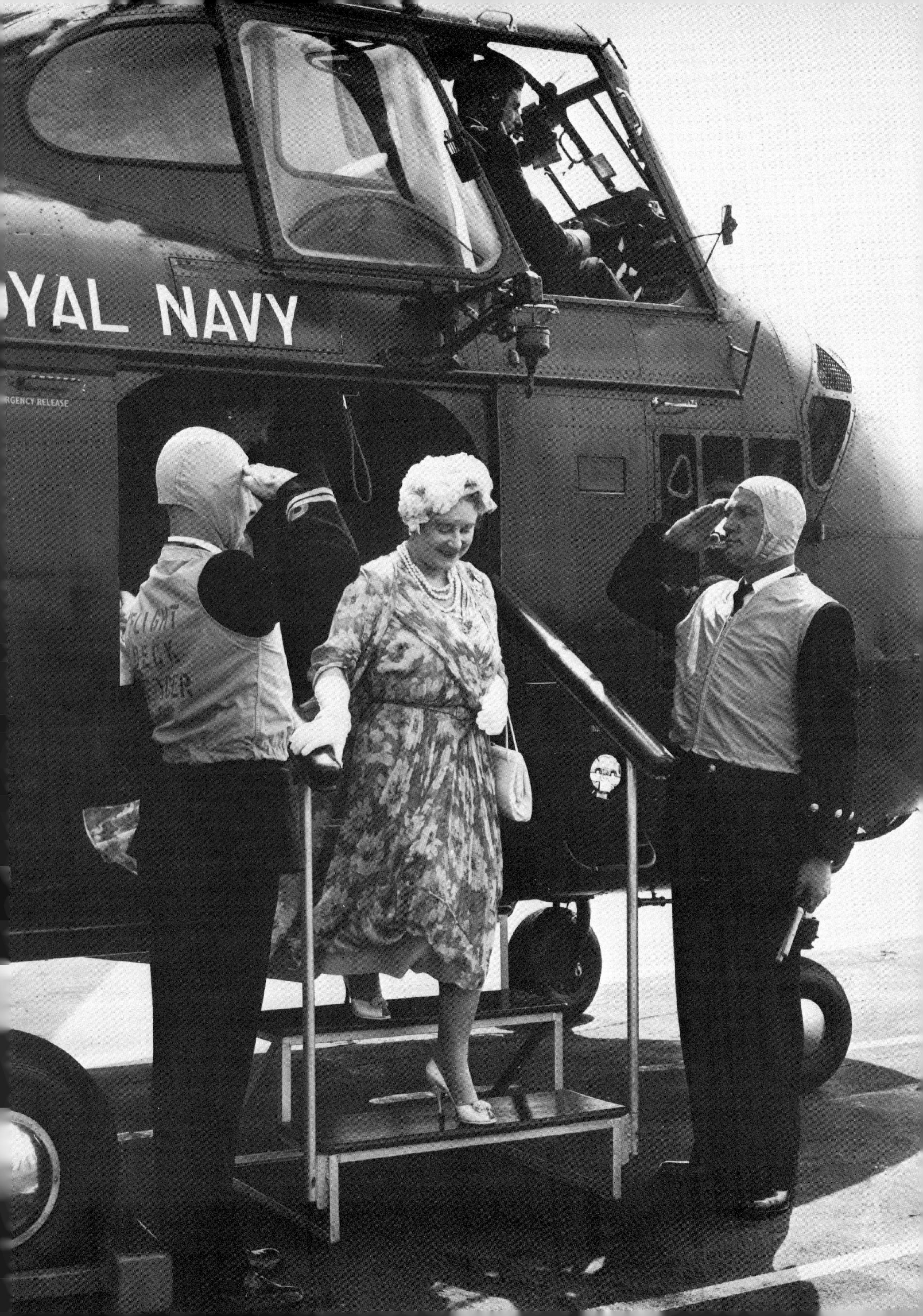

OYAL NAVY
RGENCY RELEASE

CHAPTER 6

Queen Mother

So what was going to happen to this royal lady, a loved figure on the world stage, now irrevocably cast in the role of *Parent Queen?*

That was what we wondered in the early weeks of 1952. She was still 'Her Majesty', still 'Queen Elizabeth'. But that was the elder daughter's name too, now that the young Princess had inherited the Throne and was Sovereign Lady, Britain's Head of State, Elizabeth II.

One thing that happened at once was that the King's widow, no longer royal Consort, became 'The Queen Mother'. But would there be a complete change in her life as well as her name? What part would she play, if any, she who had been so vital a figure on the national scene? Were we going to lose her? It seemed at the very first that such a loss might indeed come to pass. As devastated as Queen Victoria was when the Prince Consort died, she might, we thought, leave the world's ken now and spend her days in retirement, probably burying herself in Scotland, emerging just rarely for a family gathering or an occasional look-in at some remote Women's Institute.

The impression that she was perhaps going to disappear and put herself as far away from London as possible was strengthened when we learned that Her Majesty had suddenly purchased for herself a distant and improbable little sixteenth-century castle on the northernmost coast of the Scottish mainland, a delapidated old place that was ripe for demolition, riddled as it was with the damp and the black peat smoke of centuries: the Castle of Mey. The bleak building of pink stone was an unprepossessing house which not many people knew, even in that north-eastern corner of windswept Caithness where the abandoned dwelling stood near the shore of the stormy Pentland Firth, a dozen miles east of Thurso. It was then called – by those who could recall any name at all – Barrogill Castle. It was forlorn and for sale, but with no purchaser in prospect.

Queen Elizabeth saw the place in the early days after the King's death, when she had gone to stay with old friends in Caithness and was driving one afternoon along the lonely coast road that goes to John O'Groats. She stopped and went to have a look. Something about the house and its setting and its history at once appealed to the romantic Scot in her. Her words when she learned that the old castle was almost certainly going to be pulled down or left to a final crumbling were typically impulsive and typically sure: 'Never! It mustn't be·lost. It's part of Scotland's heritage. *I'll* buy it!' Which Her Majesty promptly did, and restored not only the name, Castle of Mey, which it had had when the noble Earl of Caithness built it four hundred years

ago, but also, gradually, the sixteenth-century appearance of the house. She then set about planning to furnish the interior to her own taste. It was several years, however, before Mey was fully recreated and, at considerable cost, made warmly habitable, and completed in style and attractiveness both inside and out. Of course the very business of building it up was a great interest and a pleasure to its royal owner. She kept *au fait* with every detail: the roofing, the laying on of water supply and electricity for power to light and heat to cook, the fitting of bathrooms, the installing of comfortable furniture, the hanging of pictures, the cleaning of outside walls and paths – and the taming of a wild garden.

Today, Mey is Queen Elizabeth's own haven, her faraway but nowadays far from forbidding retreat. She has put down roots in the Far North. She loves the mellowed and very private Castle set in that austere Caithness landscape, its population sparse, its farmlands bleak and its few trees bent halfway to the ground by the relentless wind.

She spends much of August, though not a great deal more of each year, in that little kingdom of hers; but even back in London she keeps constantly in touch with the Factor at Mey about the progress of the flock of sheep she owns on the croft adjoining the Castle, the health of the herd of Aberdeen Angus cattle, and the marketing of produce from the old garden whose fine fruit and vegetables and flowers are high-walled against the gales from the Arctic. Even at Clarence House, Her Majesty is as avid a reader of the *John O'Groat Journal* as of the London *Times*.

When she does go into residence in her Castle she enjoys every day enormously, whatever the weather. She can go about the countryside quite freely: the Caithness folk welcome a fellow countryperson with no crowding, rather with a quiet, natural warmth which does not intrude on privacy. She will chat with all and sundry during shopping expeditions in Thurso; she walks on the cliffs and sands beside her house and watches the seals at play; she gathers shells from the beach and heather from the salty moors. She has a passion for the open air and, pulling on an old felt hat and a mac, she will haul her little house party and her dogs out for some picnic excursion, rain or shine, even if it means squatting down and eating lunch in a dripping barn.

On Sunday she goes to morning service in the little whitewashed parish church of Canisbay, and afterwards may well be found holding conversation not only with the Minister but half the congregation. Up there, she 'belongs'. And Mey's special remoteness appeals to the Scot in her. Her visits are wonderfully restorative, and very precious are the clear days when she can look from a castle window and discern, far beyond the strand and the race of the sea, the outline of Kirkwall's

Opposite *Arriving on the deck of HMS* Ark Royal, *July 1958.*

Opposite, top *The Castle of Mey – the Queen Mother's home in the North on the austere Caithness coast.*

Opposite, bottom *The newly crowned Queen Elizabeth II, the Duke of Edinburgh, Queen Elizabeth The Queen Mother, Prince Charles and Princess Anne watch the Coronation Day fly-past.*

Above *The Queen Mother chats with the late Duke of Gloucester on the steps of St George's Chapel, Windsor. The occasion was the Garter Ceremony of 1954, when the Prime Minister, Sir Winston Churchill (on left), was himself installed as a Knight Companion of the Most Honourable and Noble Order.*

Right *Inspecting the Queen's Bays after their return in 1954 from a five-year tour of duty with the British Army of the Rhine.*

again, very much by popular demand. In any case, she herself in fact had no intention of abandoning duty – indeed, on reflection, how could there have been any such thing for this woman who had taught her daughters: 'Work is your devoir, the rent you pay for life.' The motto of Princes of Wales, 'I Serve', was her watchword too. Shortly after the King's death she had written: 'My only wish is that I may be allowed to continue the work that we sought to do together.' And so began her present 'third life', the best known one, the long years of joyful work in the public gaze as an energetic woman of astonishingly wide interests, an effervescent and stylish leader of the British royal scene – the perennial Queen Mother all the world has known for the past thirty years.

The first step, however, the emerging from private grief and loneliness into parade state and public scrutiny was not easy. But there was no discernible wavering in her composure when she tackled her opening engagement of the new reign in May, 1952, three months after the King's death. It was no doubt a help that the event took place in Scotland and that it concerned an army regiment of such personal and family associations – the Black Watch, whose Colonel-in-Chief she had been since 1937. This was the regiment of the Bowes-Lyon brothers; in its service Captain Fergus died in action in France in 1915. Now the First Battalion had been ordered to Korea, and Her Majesty flew from Windsor to Fife to say farewell and good luck to them. Queen Elizabeth wore black as five hundred men paraded before her, each officer wearing a dark armband of mourning. After the inspection, she went through the whole programme, meeting soldiers' relatives and old comrades, posing for official photographs, touring the quarters of officers and men. She was

ancient cathedral, pride of the main island of the Orkneys.

So the buying of that Castle of Mey in 1952 *did* give the answer to the question whether Queen Elizabeth was going to fade out – and the answer was decidedly in the negative. Mey was a blessing, not a bolt-hole. The year of the King's death was not far advanced before it was clear that she was not going into retirement. She was to be a busy person again. There was too strong a pull in the affections of the British people, she had too firm a place in the national life to be allowed to go into any sort of seclusion. Before long she was making public appearances

as marvellous with servicemen that day as she has always been, equally at home taking a dram in the Sergeants' mess as tasting the claret in the officers' dining room.

By the end of the year Her Majesty was resuming a full life of public duty and social round, busier indeed than ever before, her *élan* pleasing family and friends. It was then that she began her far travels in her own right as Queen Mother, and most of the journeys were now by air. From the first, she had been an indefatigable flyer. (She has never been either airsick or seasick in her life.) She went for a trip in the first Comet airliner only two weeks after her pilot son-in-law, Prince Philip, had made the first-ever Royal flight in a jet and she took over for a while as first pilot at forty thousand feet. No King or Queen before her had ever flown round the world when she did just that in 1958. She is very happy to be airborne.

Sadly, she was in mourning again in March 1953 when Queen Mary died at Marlborough House at the age of eighty-seven. Great though the difference in years between the two had been, the straight-backed old lady of the proprieties and the parasols had been a close friend and in many ways a fellow spirit of Queen Elizabeth ever since the days when Her Majesty, as Elizabeth Bowes-Lyon, entered the Royal Family.

Two months after Queen Mary's death, the Queen Mother, with Princess Margaret, moved her London home again, down The Mall to Clarence House this time. It was a change-about: her elder daughter, living in Buckingham Palace now that she was Queen, had lived in Clarence House as Princess Elizabeth since her marriage to the Duke of Edinburgh.

Then, on June 2, 1953 came the surpassing ceremony of her daughter's Coronation. When Elizabeth II was crowned with glittering pageantry in Westminster Abbey, the Queen Mother, wearing a magnificent train trimmed with ermine (which had belonged to Queen Mary), occupied the family's central place of honour in the front row of the Royal Gallery. It was to her side in the gallery that a small boy was slipped during the long service, a child who held Grannie's hand for a moment and then bobbed up and down for an hour, elbows on balustrade, asking excited questions as he watched all the peers and the bishops and the gold plate on the altar and the spectacular action that was taking place around his mother. The boy was Prince Charles, Duke of Cornwall (not yet Prince of Wales), then aged four, a trim little figure with slicked-down hair and a white satin suit. Queen Elizabeth smiled and whispered to him as the solemn rites went on, explaining in the clear way she has with children

Opposite, top *A hug from a small Prince Charles as his grandmother arrives back in London from her North American tour of 1954. Princess Anne waits her turn. The Queen and all the Royal Family headed the welcome at Waterloo Station.*

Opposite, bottom *Queen Elizabeth The Queen Mother in her role as Chancellor of the University of London, an office she energetically held for twenty-five years.*

Above *The Royal Chancellor walks in procession to the Albert Hall platform for the great ceremony of Presenting graduates of London University.*

Right *Having installed Peter Ustinov as Rector of Dundee University on October 20, 1968, the Queen Mother, then Chancellor, enjoys his speech.*

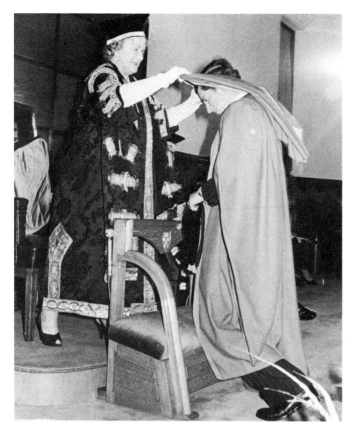

some of the things that were happening just a few yards away.

In the Abbey ritual and the long processions which flowed through London streets on Coronation Day, the brightest lights naturally fell on the new Sovereign and Prince Philip, Duke of Edinburgh. But many thousands of people on that day, as on many a day to follow, looked with particular pride and possessive remembrance on the graceful figure of Queen Elizabeth The Queen Mother. One of the many special moments of that Second of June which I remember was when the Queen and the Duke and their children, back at the Palace and out on the balcony facing a vast sea of people in front of the gates, suddenly moved apart so that there was a gap in the middle of their ranks, and into that gap the Duke turned and led out his mother-in-law. The sight of the Queen Mother was the signal for a tremendous roar of applause which obliterated even the scream of saluting aircraft streaking over the Palace.

During the following years there came many a long overseas tour. The Queen Mother was a tireless royal ambassador. She was seen in many countries: up and down Europe, across Canada and to Rhodesia several times, all over the Pacific and the Caribbean, North and Central and East Africa. In and out of ships and planes she went, much photographed, plunging straight into crowded ceremonies moments after leaving long-distance aircraft, brightly dressed and looking regal to a 'T' whether the occasion was a guard inspection, a children's gala rally, some dusty tribal review, a cold and rainswept walk, a formal reception indoors or a sweltering Government garden party.

There are memories of her sometimes unorthodox comments as she walked among crowds or stood for hours as lines of locally important people were presented to her. The sharp response and the spark of humour have always been near the surface. During the 1947 South African tour, she charmed even the occasional suspicious republican. When an old Afrikaner who had

soldiered in the Boer War told her that he 'couldn't forgive the English for what they did to my people', the Queen took the wind out of his sails with her scintillating smile and slap-bang answer: 'I do understand that so well. We in Scotland sometimes feel very much the same.'

One of the fullest tours she made after becoming Queen Mother was the one which took her for a month to North America in the autumn of 1954. She 'wowed' New York and everywhere else. It was not a State visit, but the ovations could not have been warmer. In between formal engagements she went shopping and caused a near-riot in a Fifth Avenue store where excited customers and salesgirls alike stampeded all over the floors and counters to get a sight of her. In Washington she left the White House and the Eisenhowers to look into downtown drugstores; at Annapolis the naval academy went on parade for her; and the whole Pentagon saluted as she sailed through that colossal military maze like a breath of spring in an astringent November. During the week spent in Canada, the loudest hails were of '*Vive la Reine*' when she crossed from Ontario into French Québec.

But life was not all untroubled sweetness and light. Well before she went to America the Queen Mother knew – though very possibly she wished not to contemplate the situation and believed it would go away – that her high-spirited younger daughter, Princess Margaret, twenty-four years old, wished to marry a handsome and well-liked courtier named Group Captain Peter Townsend, who had been a distinguished RAF fighter pilot in the war, had been appointed to responsible positions at Buckingham Palace by the King, and then had been brought by Queen Elizabeth into her own Household Service at Clarence House. Townsend was a commoner, an official on a royal staff, and a man fifteen years the princess's senior. However, the problem was that he was a divorced man, albeit the innocent party; and by the rules of State and Church he could not be taken in marriage by the sister of the Sovereign, the Defender of the Faith.

The situation became a front-page newspaper story; and the Group Captain was smartly posted away – to Brussels. But in 1955 the couple were meeting again, back in London, and at Clarence House too. The place was besieged by reporters and press photographers, and Townsend was chased up and down the West End, day and night, by posses of journalists fifty strong.

Though it increasingly seemed that in any case nothing could come of the romance in the face of the Queen, the Church, the Establishment, the views of the Dominions, the Royal Marriages Act's prohibitions, and the climate of morals prevailing at that time, how greatly the Queen Mother must have missed the firm and clear-sighted counsel of her late husband! It was not in her own nature to be stern or to become involved in unpleasantness. The Princess was left to make her own decision. When that decision came, it was another historic

Opposite *The massive 100-foot tower which dominates the granite grandeur of Royal Balmoral.*

Right *The Garden Room at Clarence House, Her Majesty's London home – one of the pictures taken specially at Queen Elizabeth's homes. An unfinished portrait of the Queen Mother, by Augustus John, hangs over the fireplace. The story of this portrait is told on page 148.*

Right *On the walls of the ground-floor Corridor at Clarence House hang many pictures of the racehorses of the Queen Mother's forebears. The large picture is of Coerstone, winner of the Derby and the 2,000 Guineas in 1843, and owned by Mr John Bowes. Top right is Coerstone's sire, Touchstone, with a stable lad. Below is a Stubbs painting of one of the Bowes's bay ponies.*

Left *The lovely first floor Drawing Room at Clarence House. The group portrait on the right is of the Misses Cavendish-Bentinck, one of whom was Queen Elizabeth's mother.*

Below *At the other end of the Drawing Room is a rare William-and-Mary lacquered cabinet on a silvered stand.*

Right *Her Majesty conferred the Honorary Degree of Doctor of Laws on her Private Secretary, Sir Martin Gilliat on November 24, 1977.*

Below *Upon meeting Bryn Jones, then President of the London University Students' Union, during the President of the Union's Ball on December 5, 1970 the Queen Mother, admired his hair as well as the medal.*

Opposite *In April 1959 Queen Elizabeth The Queen Mother and Princess Margaret were received by Pope John XXIII at the Vatican. Here they are leaving after their audience with His Holiness.*

Right, top *The Royal Family attending the Badminton Horse Trials – a regular date. This was in April 1956. While the Queen uses her cine-camera, the Queen Mother and Princess Margaret watch her new horse, Countryman III, take a jump.*

Right, bottom *The Queen Mother with the then Premier of New South Wales, Mr J. Cahill, at a State Reception on the evening of her arrival in Sydney in 1958. Her Majesty completely captivated the 1,000 guests with her sparkling informality.*

renunciation – though the circumstances were different from those of Edward VIII in 1936 – and sympathy went out to the young Margaret in her self-sacrifice. On October 31, 1955 Her Royal Highness issued a statement which said: '... I have decided not to marry Group Captain Peter Townsend.... Mindful of the Church's teaching that Christian marriage is indisoluble, and conscious of my duty to the Commonwealth, I have resolved to put these considerations before any others....'

The episode has passed into history, but not out of memory. Less than five years later, Princess Margaret did marry. Her engagement to a professional photographer, the talented Anthony Armstrong-Jones, was the best-kept secret and news surprise of 1960. The Princess's wedding to Mr Armstrong-Jones who was later made Earl of Snowdon, took place in Westminster Abbey on May 6. The bride was twenty-nine years old, the groom thirty. This marriage partnership, which produced two delightful children, later ran into troubled waters. It was a sadness to the Queen Mother (though as ever there was no outward sign of private feeling) when in 1976 the Princess and her husband – two artistic and volatile human beings who had been targets of considerable newspaper criticism – decided to separate. The marriage was dissolved in 1978; and at the end of that year Lord Snowdon married again. Far from being ostracized, he has continued to be welcomed at royal homes, where he has taken many admired photographs on special occasions. He it was who was invited to Kensington Palace in June, 1982, to take a series of pictures of the Princess of Wales and the newly christened Prince William: camera portraits which have been reproduced all over world.

As to Princess Margaret, the problems and the troubles which beset her in the Fifties and the two ensuing decades have caused headaches in the family but have left the Monarchy unscarred, the Queen's own family life unblemished, the Queen Mother's

Above *Her Majesty arrives in a wheelchair to launch a new liner, the 22,000-ton* Northern Star *at Newcastle-upon-Tyne in June 1961. She had cracked a bone in her left foot two weeks previously.*

Left *After the State Funeral of Sir Winston Churchill on January 30, 1965, the Royal Family, Heads of State and leading politicians gather on the steps of St Paul's.*

Opposite *In the Royal Box at Covent Garden on June 21, 1966, to attend a Gala performance in aid of the Opera House's Benevolent Fund.*

Opposite, top *Signing the Visitor's Book on board HMS Resolution, one of Britain's Polaris missile submarines. The Queen Mother toured the Clyde Submarine Base when visiting Scotland in May 1968.*

Opposite, bottom *Princess Anne, the Queen Mother, Princess Margaret and Lord Snowdon applaud during the Investiture of the Prince of Wales at Caernarvon Castle, July 2, 1969.*

Right *'Up periscope' is the command when the Queen Mother tours a mock nuclear submarine, part of the Royal Navy's exhibit at the Ideal Home Exhibition at Olympia in 1970.*

benign and busy progress through the years clearly unimpeded.

Her Majesty's own staff at Clarence House have often marvelled at the manner in which she manages to pursue so many activities, and to thrive on them – the travelling, the concert, ballet and theatre dates, the racegoing, the collecting of pictures and *objets d'art*, the walking, the fishing, the consuming devotion to dogs, the interest in gardens, the reading, letter-writing, *hours* of telephoning, the family gatherings, and the catching up with favourite television programmes whenever outside duties allow.

All that and the official meetings and attendances too. She is President or Patron of three hundred organizations. She is Colonel-in-Chief of a dozen regiments, Commander-in-Chief of all the Women's Services. She is the head of orders of chivalry, holder of many honorary degrees, and a Master of the Bench of the Middle Temple. From the lists of hospitals, churches, charities and assorted societies which have her official patronage, a random selection discloses the Church Army, the Bible Reading Fellowship, the College of Speech Therapists, the British Home and Hospital for Incurables, the Injured Jockeys Fund, the Grand Military Race Meeting, the National Trust, the Royal College of Music, the Royal School of Needlework, the Dachshund Club, the Keep Britain Tidy Group, and the Women's Institutes of Windsor, Sandringham, Crathie and Birkhall.

She has a special place in history as a university Chancellor. When she took her last Foundation Day ceremony in December 1980 she had been Chancellor of the University of London for a full twenty-five years. She gave to that position a whole-hearted

and sustained devotion which was unique and which made her uniquely loved.

It is hard to think of any sort of university event she did not attend in those years, any facet of activity she has not personally examined, any college of this great complex of student activity which she has not explored. Schools and faculties, clubs and halls of residence, institutes for past-graduate study – she knows them all. The special academic occasions appeal to her sense of tradition and order, her knowledge of learning and her own quick intelligence. And the outdoor events strike the chords of sporting life that are within her. In boathouse and pavilions men still recall her sprightly encouragement to Varsity crews from the banks of a windblown Thames at Henley. She herself presided over a celebration dinner in 1963 when the University boat club won the Grand Challenge Cup for the first time; and the First Eight boat was proud to bear her name. By the time she relinquished the Chancellorship, over three hundred official visits to London University were in the calendars, more than a dozen a year.

Her conduct of the imposing Foundation Day ceremonies when honorary degrees are bestowed at Senate House was always a model of grace, her performance at each twice-yearly Presentation Day in the Royal Albert Hall astonishing in stamina and resilience. The Presentations are marathon royal duties. The hall is crowded to the roof; the platform a blaze of academic gowns and hoods because it is solid with the professorial Great Ones; and in a huge chair at the centre of the stage we have seen, time after time, Her Majesty the Chancellor in robes of black and gold. She speaks her 'charge to the

Graduates', and then, smiling and straight-backed, head high, she 'nods through' the new graduates one by one, two thousand young men and young women who have gained their first degree. For over two hours they pass before her in never-ending line, each giving a bow or a curtsey as his or her name is called, each receiving from the lady in the chair a smile and encompassing gaze of individual recognition, special to each person and never forgotten. And after all that, there has been another task: the presentation of high degrees. Enough for one day, you might think. But after that we would behold the royal Chancellor at the Abbey or St Paul's for a long Presentation Day service, still seeming extraordinarily spry.

Her Majesty's university activities and holdings of high academic office have not been confined to London. She was the first Chancellor of the University of Dundee at its establishment in 1967, and she held that position – to her own and Scotland's delight – for ten years, regularly attending all Dundee's major occasions.

But it is, of course, London's university which has a great kaleidoscope of memories of its famous Chancellor. Some of these recollections are of a graceful lady in official hat and gown, others of a crinolined fairy figure floating expertly round a ballroom floor, lighter on her feet than anyone present, and entirely *en rapport* with the young men about her

Legends have come down from some of the students' dances

Above *A royal visit to London's East End on July 12, 1972, to inspect gardens of Greater London Council tenants in Hackney. At one house on the Frampton Park Estate a young man gets his personal portrait, when the Queen Mother, spotting him, stops to pose.*

Left *The young King of Sweden, Carl XVI Gustav, with Queen Elizabeth The Queen Mother and the late Earl Mountbatten of Burma.*

Having established a style which particularly suited her early in the reign of the King, Queen Elizabeth has remained faithful to it ever since. In this most becoming photograph, taken in the early 1960s, Her Majesty arrives at a function wearing a dark outfit, a rare occurrence.

Left *The keen interest shown here was, not surprisingly, at Badminton. The Queen Mother's critical appraisal was matched by young Princess Anne's.*

Below *Visits to schools have been much enjoyed dates in Her Majesty's diary, and the royal visitor is always accorded an enthusiastic reception by the boys or girls and parents. Here the Queen Mother is at the Leys School, Cambridge, on June 6, 1961.*

Opposite *All eyes are on Princess Anne as she hands her wedding bouquet to her bridesmaid, Lady Sarah Armstong-Jones, at the beginning of the marriage ceremony in Westminster Abbey on November 14, 1973.*

Above *The Queen Mother leads other members of the Royal Family into Westminster Hall on May 4, 1977, for the presentation of addresses by both Houses of Parliament on the occasion of Queen Elizabeth II's Silver Jubilee.*

Opposite, top *Prince Andrew and Prince Edward accompany their popular grandmother as she rides through the London streets on June 7, 1977 – Jubilee Day.*

Opposite, bottom *The congregation in St Paul's Cathedral during the Jubilee Day Thanksgiving Service. Leading figures of the nation and Commonwealth attended.*

which she used to attend. There are tales of appreciative but apprehensive youths taking dancing lessons against the probability that they would find themselves on the ballroom floor partnering the gossamer performer; stories of a pair of men's white gloves getting more and more perspiration-soaked as the evening went on and as they were passed from boy to boy when *his* time came to dance with the Chancellor; and especially the story of the earnestly nervous young President of the Students' Union, a trier, but one whose terpsichorean antics suggested that he posessed two left feet. Dutifully taking the floor with the radiant royal figure in the diamond-studded gown, he stumbled round in a state of alarm whilst his partner featly avoided the heavier kicks on the ankles and smiled the while as though blissfully in the arms of an expert of the waltz. Presently the young man found that he was doing rather better than he had imagined, such was the skill of the lady. It was, however, a rough ride as the two twirled and bumped along – but a dance which made the boy (who later became a QC and an MP) a Queen Mum Worshipper ever since, for in the middle of it all Her Majesty murmured into his ear: 'Don't worry, Mr President, you haven't knocked my tiara off yet.'

It remains to be seen whether Princess Anne, who was chosen as London University's Chancellor after an election contest in 1981, will make the same joyous mark on this great centre of education as her grandmother has done. She has no easy task in following such a star.

Queen Elizabeth has of course been a physically fit and vigorous person. In the Fifties and Sixties there were occasional stumbles, a twisted ankle, fractures of a small bone in the foot. She made quick recoveries – and continued to wear high heels.

She underwent an appendectomy in King Edward VII's Hospital for Officers in 1964 – and almost immediately afterwards was sitting up and receiving friends, smile in place and face and hair immaculate.

Two years later she was in the same place for something more serious (though nobody who saw her, bright as ever at a Women's Voluntary Service reception a few hours before, could have had any idea of the prospect she faced). The prospect was a major abdominal operation, and this was carried out on December 10, 1966 – a date precisely thirty years after the Abdication which made her Queen – and she had to remain in hospital during all that Christmas and New Year season, whilst a tide of visiting relatives and letters, telegrams, flowers and other gifts from people all over the world nearly swamped the hospital. The tributes overflowed from her room, and for some time the wards and corridors of 'Sister Agnes's', as this hospital is familiarly known, looked like part of Chelsea Flower Show. The spirit and the interests of the patient did not flag even during the weeks of uncomfortable recuperation. One afternoon, her bedroom became the excited Royal Box of a racehorse owner as, through BBC television coverage specially rescheduled for her, she watched three of her horses win prizes at a Sandown Park meeting.

After the long troublesome hospital experience for a woman of sixty-six, an easing of the pace of life might have been expected. But no, by the end of January 1967, she was out and about and busy again, remarkably recovered, full of go, avid for travel. And so she has continued to be, vital and radiant (as was demonstrated in the startling hours at that same hospital late in 1982 – which our story will recall in a later chapter).

Inevitably, the sunshine of her Queen Mother years has also had its clouds: losses of relatives and friends. The cruellest stroke was the death in 1961 of her brother Sir David Bowes-Lyon – David, the twin-Benjamin of her childhood, who had remained close and dear to his sister throughout adult life. It was he who had lived, with his wife Rachel, at St Paul's Walden Bury, the childhood home, and it was his habit there to get up early each weekday morning and arrange the day's work in his garden before leaving for London. He died, at fifty-nine, whilst on holiday at his royal sister's Deeside house, Birkhall, but they buried him at the Hertfordshire home beside the lawns and enchanted woodlands where a small Elizabeth and David had played together fifty years before. (Her Majesty still visits his widow at St Paul's for a quiet, nostalgic week-end each year.)

The Queen Mother's brother-in-law, the Duke of Gloucester, the royal brother who had been next in age to her husband, died in 1974, two years after his elder son, Prince William, had been killed in an air race.

A few months before that tragic ending of a young life, a much older and once a much more eminent Prince died in Paris – the Duke of Windsor, quondam king, the man who had altered Elizabeth Bowes-Lyon's life when he ceased to be Edward VIII. He was almost seventy-eight years old. The Royal Air Force flew his body back to England and to a lying-in-state at Windsor; his widowed Duchess followed and came to London, bidden to stay at Buckingham Palace. Only once, five years before had the Queen Mother met her, briefly, as her brother-in-law's wife. The occasion was the quick visit of the Duke and Duchess to London to see the Queen unveil a plaque to Queen Mary's memory in the wall of her old home, Marlborough House. Now, the encounter was at a sombre family gathering on

June 5, 1972, in the banner-hung magnificence of the Chapel of
St George at Windsor Castle, where the once High and Mighty
Prince was accorded all the obsequies of majesty before the
private burial in royal ground at Frogmore.

But it is new lives, new alliances, new marriages and the births
of new generations of the Royal Family that have been the
highlights and the happy memories of Queen Elizabeth's recent
decades. The celebrations and the great ceremonies – these have
been among her chief joys. The sight of Her Majesty herself, to
400,000,000 television viewers of the event all over the world,
was one of the most pleasing figures of the assembled clan on
July 1, 1969, when pageantry flowed through Caernarvon
Castle at the traditional Investing of her grandson as Prince of
Wales. In 1972, her reigning daughter's Silver Wedding twenty-
four years after her own – was another proud moment for the
Queen Mother. Then there was the marriage of her granddaughter, Princess Anne, to Captain Mark Phillips, during the
ensuing year; the Queen's fiftieth-birthday parties in 1976; and
in 1977 the long series of celebrations to mark the twenty-fifth
anniversary of the Queen's reign, a Silver Jubilee which was as
uplifting an experience for the Sovereign's mother as it was for
the Monarch herself and the whole nation.

A particular pleasure of the year 1977 was the Jubilee Year
Baby, the son – christened Peter Mark Andrew and bearing no
royal title – who was born to Princess Anne and Captain Phillips
on November 15, four years and a day after their wedding. Here
was the first of a new generation of the Royal Family, making
the Queen a grandmother at the age of fifty-one and bringing to
the Queen Mother her latest style – Great-Grannie.

The birth of a great-grand-*daughter* came in 1981: Princess
Anne's second child, called Zara Anne Elizabeth. Prince
William, first cousin of Master Peter and Miss Zara, was to
appear little more than twelve months later – and he, Prince
William of Wales, was to be, incomparably, the most important
baby of this newest generation.

But before the story of that arrival, there is much to tell – of an
historic engagement and marriage and a royal grandmother's
part in it. And, even before that, other joys, and some sorrows,
along Queen Elizabeth's road must be related. In particular,
one great ceremony heralded the 1980s.

Opposite *The Queen Mother leaves St Paul's Cathedral on Jubilee
Day escorted by the Prince of Wales in full dress uniform as Colonel
of the Welsh Guards, and followed by Prince Andrew and the then
young Prince Edward.*

Above *In the royal procession back to Buckingham Palace on
June 7, Queen Elizabeth rode with three grandsons.*

Below *From the balcony of Buckingham Palace the Queen and her
family wave to the thousands who have come to see them on Jubilee
Day. (From the left) Prince Charles, Prince Edward, Prince
Andrew, the late Earl Mountbatten, the Queen, Prince Philip,
Captain Mark Phillips, Princess Anne, the Queen Mother and
Princess Margaret.*

CHAPTER 7

Into the Eighties

IN HER public life, the principal prelude to Her Majesty's honoured Eighties was a day at Dover in Kent, a day memorable for its uncivil rain, which however failed to remove the shine from Queen Elizabeth's installation as Constable of Dover Castle and Lord Warden and Admiral of the Cinque Ports, an office never before bestowed on a woman. August 1, 1979 was the date. The new Admiral has described it as 'one of the happiest days of my life.'

For this historic introduction into a post which had been continuously occupied since before the reign of William the Conqueror, she took three grandchildren with her: Prince Edward, and Princess Margaret's son and daughter, Viscount Linley and Lady Sarah Armstrong-Jones. They sailed to Dover in the Royal Yacht *Britannia* and, once ashore, received the full treatment of guards of honour, gun salutes, pipe music, and State carriage processions escorted by Household Cavalry.

The chief ceremony took place in a marquee at the Ancient Priory of St Martin before a thousand people, headed by the robed Barons and mayors and august representatives of the Cinque Ports (originally Sandwich, Dover, Hythe, Romney, and Hastings, but now a Confederation of fourteen towns stretching round England's south-east corner to Margate and the approaches to the Thames).

In both the downpours and the brief bright intervals of better weather, big crowds of people in the streets of the port cheered the processions and the royal lady they carried. Several times during the day's events, Her Majesty went on foot among the spectators, making specially for lines of old folk in wheelchairs and then to ranks of children, emerging almost embowered in posies and bouquets. Rain or no rain, Queen Elizabeth looked every inch the radiant person they all knew and wanted to salute for themselves. There were official speeches of course. Judge Darling, of the Court of Admiralty, said there had probably never been a Lord Warden held in such high esteem; and the Archbishop of Canterbury was in no doubt that 'we all owe her more than can ever be repaid.'

For her part, the royal admiral swore 'to maintain the franchises, liberties, customs and usages of the ports.' And since that day she has been characteristically arduous in making visits to her Kent and Sussex 'realms'.

When you looked at this Queen on the festive day it was hard to believe that she was within three days of her seventy-ninth birthday. She had been energetic all year. Earlier in the summer she had made yet another of her spirited progresses through Canada. This time the scenes were Toronto and Halifax, Nova Scotia – 'the Royal Province of New Scotland', as she called it. The official routines were arduous – even a young person would probably have found them so – but she as usual seemed to be ashine with joy all the way to the last late night.

But that same year brought sorrow. Twenty-six days after the Dover inauguration, Earl Mountbatten, the Royal Family's 'Uncle Dickie', who was almost exactly the same age as Queen

Opposite *Smiling in the rain – at Dover, where the new Lord Warden of the Cinque Ports took office on August 1, 1979.*

Right *Canada has long been a favourite country for Queen Elizabeth. Her most recent visits have been in 1979 and 1981. Nova Scotia and Toronto have usually been in the itineraries. Here she has landed at a military airfield near Halifax, to present Maritime Command colours, but typically she goes first to see the waiting children. The 1981 tour took in bicentenary celebrations at Niagara-on-the-Lake, Ontario.*

Elizabeth, was murdered by an Irish terrorists' bomb placed in his boat near his holiday house in County Sligo. As always when harsh personal loss came, Her Majesty showed little outward sign of what must have been sharpest shock and grief. It was left to the Prince of Wales, at the Mountbatten memorial service in St Paul's, poignantly to express the family's deep deprival. To a hushed congregation, he spoke with rare public anger of the 'mindless cruelty' of the killers and of the 'vulnerability of civilised democracy and freedom to the kind of subhuman extremism which blows people up when it feels like it.'

That was an expression of revulsion and horror which many people must have remembered later, on the July day of 1982

Above *Princess Michael of Kent and her husband (left) join the race-going scene and regular occupants of the Royal Box at Epsom. A picture on Derby Day, 1980.*

Left *'Monty' is ten feet tall as Queen Elizabeth in Whitehall unveils the statue of Field Marshall Viscount Montgomery of Alamein. This was June 6, 1980, thirty-six years after the D-day landings of World War Two.*

Opposite *Her Majesty, with the traditional nosegay, leaves Westminster Abbey at the head of the Royal Almonry procession, after the Royal Maundy service and distribution of alms in 1970.*

Right Approaching the steps of St George's Chapel, Windsor, to attend the annual Garter service. On the right of the Queen Mother is the late Duke of Gloucester.

Below In Edinburgh in the robes of Lady of the Order of the Thistle, Scotland's Most Ancient and Most Noble Order of Chivalry, which was revived by King James VII in 1687.

Opposite, top The Queen Mother making the traditional distribution of shamrock at a St Patrick's Day parade.

Opposite, bottom The Armed Forces combine to furnish a guard of honour for the visitor to the Royal Tournament in 1975.

when London experienced the brutality of IRA explosions which slaughtered soldiers and civilians in Knightsbridge and Regent's Park – dastardly acts occurring during a week when the world was already rocked by news of most serious lapses in Palace security, disclosed by the incredible intrusion of a housebreaker who was able to reach the very bedside of the Sovereign herself. The incident shocked the nation. Happily, Clarence House – which has been the Queen Mother's London home for thirty years – was, although so near to Buckingham Palace, an oasis of calm during the dramas of that week.

In short, Clarence House does not change. It gives no appearance of a guarded fortress. It is a royal home and headquarters, a very pleasant one. To the visitor, the house has a uniquely serene and charming atmosphere, graceful in a gracious age. It is physically attached to St James's Palace, but is a separate domain, a little kingdom of its own. It takes its character from its occupant. Her Majesty has made it a home of taste and elegance, bright, welcoming, rich in massed flowers and in fine collections of pictures and *objets d'art*.

Externally, however, the building in which the Queen Mother lives is at first sight undistinguished – and difficult for the public to see. Even if tourists could view it over the high walls they would behold an architectural jumble. No wonder. From a sixteenth-century outbuilding of St James's, John Nash only partly rebuilt the place for the Duke of Clarence who became King William IV. Much of the house as it stands today was created bit by bit late last century when it was occupied by Queen Victoria's second son, 'Alfie', Duke of Edinburgh. Later, the old Queen's seventh offspring, the Duke of Connaught, had it for *his* house for the first forty years of this century. After the Second World War it was the first family home of the present Queen when, as Princess Elizabeth, she had married the Duke of Edinburgh of the present day. Princess Anne was born there.

All that is ageing history. In modern times, the world knows that 'Clarence House, St James's, London S.W.' is the official address of Queen Elizabeth The Queen Mother. Through its doors, during 1980 poured birthday cakes and an indescribable variety of other gifts, and assorted items of mail and telegrams in tens of thousands. From the highest to the humblest in the land, people wanted to say thank-you and to wish her well. For 1980 was The Year of the Eightieth Birthday.

Widespread celebrations of the event began months before the actual anniversary, August 4, and an augmented but still overworked staff at the House were dealing with the avalanches of presents, letters and greeting cards by the sackful, from all over the world, almost until Christmas.

Opposite *The Queen Mother leaving St Paul's Cathedral after the Silver Jubilee Thanksgiving Service. With her, as she waves in greeting, are Prince Charles (right) and the Princes Andrew and Edward (left).*

Right, above *One of the Special-Birthday year's visits took the Queen Mother to the Royal Tournament again. A truly military cake was the surprise item behind the scenes. Regimental names associated with Her Majesty were in the decorative icing.*

Right, below *Her own corgis, Geordie and Blackie, were inevitably in the 1980 pictures.*

Left *Grandeur of setting and assembled guests beneath the dome of St Paul's – another Eightieth Birthday picture, showing the Queen Mother, the Queen and Prince Philip at the front of the congregation. The City sword lies before the Sovereign.*

Opposite, left *In her own Scotland during the same memorable year, the Queen Mother went to dinner at the Palace of Holyroodhouse. Her sash was of Royal Stewart tartan.*

Opposite, right *Queen Elizabeth was the Prime Minister's guest at a dinner in her honour in November 1980. Mrs Thatcher welcomes Her Majesty as she arrives at Number 10 Downing Street*

Of all the salutes, the chief one was the great Service of Thanksgiving in St Paul's Cathedral – and even that took place on July 15, more than three weeks in advance of the precise date. It was an unforgettable occasion, both national pageant and personal gathering. Had the form of the anniversary been left to the lady herself, she would doubtless have voted for no inordinate fuss, though certainly a private party with friends and descendants. Her family, and indeed the world, had other ideas. Naturally, those were the plans which prevailed. So the Fifteenth of July produced a golden day of tribute and ceremonial in a gift-wrapped London, its beflagged pavements chock-a-block with people of all ages, anxious to cheer and wave to a special person as she rode by in an open State landau, with the Prince of Wales sitting beside her, on her way from Buckingham Palace through Westminster and the City to the historic hilltop Cathedral.

There was no mistaking that it was Grannie's Day. Throughout the programme, the Queen Mother had an unprecedented pride of place over everyone, including her daughter, the Monarch. Very deliberately, the Queen placed her mother to the fore. So she and the Duke of Edinburgh and the whole of the rest of the Family – Princess Margaret, Prince Andrew and Prince Edward, the royal Gloucesters and Kents with their children – came first to the church in a stream of spectacular horses and carriages. They waited inside (all save Sovereign and Consort), in their seats beneath Sir Christopher Wren's vast dome, whilst the Star of the Occasion was making

her special, separate progress along the processional route. All the others of the Royal Family had been traditionally accompanied in their coaches by mounted troopers in full-dress uniform of plumes and shining cuirasses. Splendid enough. But Queen Elizabeth's procession had the extra touch: by her daughter's command, she was given a complete *Sovereign's Escort* of Household Cavalry.

And it was the Sovereign who came out and waited on the steps of St Paul's to greet her mother and then to stand back, accepting second place, as Queen Elizabeth stood waving to the people who were now massed, a clamorous kaleidoscope of humanity, on every inch of Ludgate Hill and at every window in sight.

The Queen Mother was herself a picture, dressed in the style the world knew and hoped-for, smiling from a mist of ostrich feathers and sapphire chiffon. Her dress had diaphanous floating panels which streamed out like banners as she waved, defiantly bare-armed on a day that was hardly summery and had in fact sent many people into overcoats. But there she was, on parade, impervious as ever to chilly winds.

Within the Cathedral, scene and service were splendid but not starchy. Great personages of the realm were to be discerned in the congregation of 2,700 souls – Officers of State and Captains of Arms, Commonwealth statesmen, ambassadors and political leaders, lords and ladies. Plus the resplendent colonels of seventeen regiments of which Her Majesty is Colonel-in-Chief or Honorary Colonel.

She personally, of course, had applied a hand to the guest-list, perhaps taking the necessary diplomats and directors and duchesses for granted, and had made sure that invitations went out to a good many persons who, whilst not publicly known, had been in her service and become her friends. Thus one noticed – all well placed in the transepts, retired gardeners from Windsor and Balmoral, a lady who 'does the flowers' at Clarence House, former footmen, nurserymaids of other years, cooks and pages still in royal service, secretaries and chauffeurs – and her present staffs: everyone, indeed, with ten years service or more. One or two retainers from royal Deeside seemed well to the fore. From the far Castle of Mey, the housekeeper and her husband had been brought down all the 700 miles to London. Present also, and still bright-eyed to witness the celebration, was an old lady who half a century before had been the cook at 145 Piccadilly when Her Majesty was Duchess of York.

The service was described by the Archbishop of Canterbury, Dr Runcie, as 'the most beautiful I've taken.' It was interdenominational, with the Moderator of the Church of Scotland reading the lesson and Cardinal Hume saying prayers. The trumpet fanfares were faultless, the music fine, the singing full-throated. One remembered smiles rather than solemnity, for all the magnificence of the copes of the clergy and the stiffly sentinel figures of bodyguard Yeomen and Gentlemen-at-Arms.

As to the central figure of it all, she positively glowed. Somehow, when she sat at the head of the assembly and twice walked the nave, Queen Elizabeth's smile seemed to embrace everybody. As she passed, you felt that the look was personally for *you*. She is like that.

Dr Runcie – we were new to the Primate's distinctive style in his addresses at that time – spoke felicitously from the pulpit of her famous face, bearing 'it's share of dignity which comes from suffering, but which is full of life, affection and cheerfulness and a zest for new things and people. . . . Royalty puts a human face on the operations of Government; and the Queen Mother helps us to feel that being a citizen of this country is not just being an entry on a central computer, but is being a member of a family.' The Archbishop continued: 'It is difficult to fall in love with committees or policies, but the Queen Mother has shown a human face which has called out affection and loyalty and the sense of *belonging*, without which a nation loses its heart.'

The nation 'lost its heart', in a quite different sense of the phrase, when the birthday itself came, on August 4, 1980 – lost its heart, demonstrably, to the royal lady. Crowds engulfed the approaches to her house that morning. They cheered and they sang and they waited. The Welsh Guards marched past, their band playing 'Happy Birthday'. Then the crowds had their reward. Queen Elizabeth came out onto her balcony. But Clarence House's balcony is small and remote and not easy to watch. So presently the big wooden gates in the garden wall swung open, and out on the pavement stepped the focus of attention. She stood there, flashing the wanted smile right and left. Both daughters were with her. Over the road, children ducked under the crowd-barriers and rushed up to pile bunches of flowers and lovingly home-made birthday cards into Her Majesty's arms.

Salutes of guns boomed from batteries in Hyde Park and at the Tower of London. From Parliament, a deputation representing both Lords and Commons came with stately tread to Clarence House to present an Address of birthday congratulation.

That night, as less formal celebration parties were taking

place up and down the land, festival bonfires blazed on Kent and Sussex coasts. Queen Elizabeth herself, accompanied by her family, chose to mark the anniversary by going to the Royal Opera House, Covent Garden, to receive the honour of a special triple-bill ballet performance, which included the world première of *Rhapsody*, a new work by her friend, the seventy-five-year-old Sir Frederick Ashton. When the grand finale of the gala evening came, silver petals rained down from the theatre ceiling, and company and audience joined in spontaneous musical salute to ballet's Number One Patron.

She did not go straight home after that, but joined the dancers and Opera House staff at their own party on stage. There was birthday cake and champagne. Heart-shaped balloons floated round the royal head. The message embellished on them was simply: 'We love you, Queen Mum.'

The 'Mum', the Golden Grannie, looked extraordinarily young, light of foot, face unlined, blue eyes shining. She made the arithmetic of the years seem absurd. She was still Royalty Rejuvenated. Her mother-in-law Queen Mary had hated being an octogenarian. 'Dreadful bore, getting old,' she used to say. But *this* Dowager was something quite different. She left 'the Garden' on Birthday Night with wings on her heels and a buoyant hope in her heart for activities still to come.

It was not that Her Majesty was living in some selfish dream-world. She knew well enough that the Eighties through which she and the twentieth century were now beginning to move were going to be years of challenge and hardship, problems and danger, for the nation and the world. She has never been unaware of or indifferent to life around her, though brightness amid gloom has always been her way. 'Chin up' would be too crude a way of labelling her attitude to the harsh realities of this

Opposite One of the century's most delightful camera portraits of a mother and her daughters. The camera artistry of Norman Parkinson.

Above Attendance at the annual Highland Gathering at Braemar is a late-summer 'must' in the diaries of the Royal Family, by then on holiday on Deeside. Here, Lady Sarah Armstrong-Jones has joined the Prince of Wales and their grandmother in the Royal Pavilion.

or any other decade; but it is her philosophy that to complain and despair, to sit around and behave miserably, does not help anybody or anything.

So she pressed on with her own work and her own life, a shrewd, grateful and inspiring Public Figure, a successful career woman, with royalty as her business.

In that business, happiness for other people is, without affectation, happiness for her. And, being a 'family person', close to her own descendants and particularly to her first grandson, she must have been longing to see Prince Charles happily settling in marriage and looking forward to a family life of his own: he was well into his thirty-second year, and the world's most eligible bachelor.

There was not much longer to wait and wonder. It came to pass that in the very next year, 1981, dreams came true, romance blossomed, a delightful and instantly popular choice was made, and the House of Windsor received a lovely young Princess of Wales.

CHAPTER 8

A Wedding to Remember

YEARS OF speculation about Prince Charles and marriage ended in a moment of matchless theatre in the heart of Buckingham Palace itself. It was eleven o'clock on the morning of February 24, 1981. Queen Elizabeth the Second had just arrived at the dais in the ballroom, ready to carry out an investiture. She stood beneath the lights, a rosy figure in the centre of her courtiers, facing an audience composed of relatives of those men and women she was about to honour, and gave the customary nod – and a more than customary smile – to her Lord Chamberlain to start the ceremony. But instead of calling the name of the first person to be knighted, Lord Maclean stepped forward and read this statement to the hushed guests:

'The Queen has asked me to let you know that an announcement is being made at this moment in the following terms:

'It is with the greatest pleasure that the Queen and the Duke of Edinburgh announce the betrothal of their beloved son, the Prince of Wales, to the Lady Diana Spencer, daughter of the Earl Spencer and the Honourable Mrs Shand Kydd.'

Applause burst out; the Guards orchestra in the minstrels' gallery struck up a lively tune; and Her Majesty began the investiture. Simultaneously, the words of the historic statement, and the news that the engagement would be followed by a wedding in July, was being flashed round the world.

The world was already familiar with the fiancée's name. She was 'Lady Di' as far as the popular newspapers were concerned. Cameramen and gossip-column writers had been hot on her trail since the previous autumn, betting with mounting confidence that she was going to be Prince Charles's wife. But nothing was sure, nothing official. They could have been wrong – until that investiture morning. Then, from the moment the engagement was revealed, Diana Spencer became the most photographed woman in the world.

Yet she had not been one of 'the Prince's girl friends', chased and chatted about through the years. Until a few months earlier this young lady, aged only nineteen, had never been in the

public gaze. She was unheard-of and unlikely. But now, as newspapers and magazines excitedly disclosed the face and history of a stunningly fresh English beauty, it seemed amazing that His Royal Highness had ever looked at anybody else – and even more extraordinary that she had been under his very nose for some years. He was marrying 'the girl next door'.

For Lady Diana was born and spent her childhood years at Park House, which was then her parents' home and which happened to be on the Sandringham estate. She and her sisters played and swam with neighbours from the Big House: a young Prince Andrew and a young Prince Edward were among their friends at holiday times. The connection was not new: the Queen's family and the Spencers had lines of ancestry in common. The Queen Mother, often at Sandringham, knew and liked the Spencer girls; and both Diana's grandmothers – the

Opposite July 29, 1981. *The Archbishop of Canterbury, Dr Runcie blesses the bride and groom, as the Heir to the Throne is married in St Paul's Cathedral.*

Right *Before she became a Princess, before her betrothal, the then Lady Diana Spencer had often to dash from her car to her London flat with a whole corps of press cameramen in pursuit.*

late Countess Spencer and Lady Fermoy – were ladies-in-waiting to Her Majesty.

So this once-unknown Diana, today's Princess of Wales, did however possess a special familiarity with the world of royalty.

She belonged to a noble family very old and very English, able to trace blood relationship from Stuart kings. Ancestors had served their Sovereigns. And her own father, before he succeeded to the earldom and its stately home, Althorp near Northampton, was, as Viscount Althorp, an equerry to King George VI and then to the present Queen in the first three years of her reign. Another link with the Palace was forged when one of her sisters, Lady Jane, married Mr Robert Fellowes, the Queen's Assistant Private Secretary.

The other married sister, Lady Sarah McCorquodale, claims to have brought Prince Charles and Lady Diana into adult consciousness of each other in 1977 when the Prince was one of

the party at a pheasant shoot on her husband's estate. They met on that occasion in the middle of a muddy ploughed field. Diana was sixteen. His Royal Highness has recalled, in more recent times, thinking: 'What a very jolly, amusing and attractive girl.' Lady Diana's phrase about *him*, 'Pretty amazing,' was succeeded in the next year or two by expressions unmistakably rapt, though said in confidence to close friends. As time went on, the ploughed field encounter was followed by other meetings, occasionally at Balmoral.

The fact seems to be that the Charles-and-Diana romance was something which grew gradually, and with increasing joy and certainty. Some years before, His Royal Highness had said: 'Whoever my wife is, she'll have to face a demanding position in public life; she'll have to be a pretty special and unusual person. But when I marry I shall marry for love.' And he did just that. This royal match was of the couple's own choosing. Nothing

Opposite *Girl in a boat. An
album snap of a very young
Lady Diana on 1970 summer
holiday at Itchenor, Sussex.*

Right *The famous smile, the
hat, the gloves, the figure
everyone knows and admires –
the epitome of royal grace and
charm.*

Below *As part of the
celebrations for the Queen's
Silver Jubilee, the Royal
Family attend a Gala Ballet at
Covent Garden in June 1977.*

Below *The scene in St Paul's Cathedral during the service held on June 7, 1977, on the occasion of the Silver Jubilee of Her Majesty The Queen. Standing beside the Queen is the Duke of Edinburgh. On either side of the aisle, the Queen Mother and the Prince of Wales are at the centre of the distinguished congregation's Royal front row.*

Opposite *A wave to the world's press as Lady Diana is driven from Buckingham Palace to the haven of Clarence House on Engagement Day, Tuesday, February 24, 1981.*

diplomatically arranged about it, nothing dictated mainly by dynastic contriving, as often happened in royal circles in past ages. That is what Britain liked about the engagement and the marriage. It was two people in love. There was widespread approbation and excitement over the new royal 'pin-up', the delightfully fresh and unspoiled piece of national property which had been acquired: Lady Diana Spencer.

Details about her were eagerly being sought by the public in 1981; her story was printed over and over again. She was the third and youngest daughter of the eighth Earl Spencer and his first wife, formerly the Honourable Frances Roche and now, in her second marriage, Mrs Shand Kydd, whose husband had farming and business interests in Scotland and in Australia. Lady Diana's parents separated when she was six. Her father married again, and the present Countess Spencer is Raine, formerly Lady Dartmouth, and daughter of the writer of romantic fiction, Barbara Cartland.

Students of the early history of the Princess of Wales soon discovered that Diana Spencer was one of those young ladies who endear themselves, not so much by classroom or playing-fields prowess as by their innate character – in this case, cheerful self-reliance, sweet temper, love of animals kept as pets, and spontaneous kindness to younger pupils as she became a school senior. She adored babies and small children. She was, in one headmistress's words, 'Marvellous at any kind of social work. Certainly she liked young toddlers, but she had a very genuine rapport with the old people she used to visit and to help. Very considerate; and she just liked doing that sort of work. She thought of others before she thought of herself.'

Princess though she now is, her character has not altered. Even in the heady excitements of the first weeks of her betrothal there were signs of that. One day she was walking past a line of people who had come to get a glimpse of her when she noticed that an old lady in the middle of the crowd was blind. All she could do was sit and listen. Diana Spencer stopped her progress, went across to the crowd and put her left hand into the blind woman's lap, so that the old hands could *feel* the diamonds-and-sapphire engagement ring.

It was perhaps hardly surprising that in her late teens Lady Diana had taken to working with children. She got a job as an assistant teacher at a kindergarten in Pimlico, London. She often wore informal sweaters and slacks – though whatever she wore, the clothes were fashionable and she looked very eye-catching. She liked the newest styles of the Chelsea smart-set's jackets and scarves; she liked now and then to eat-out in some good but tucked-away South Kensington restaurant, but was never one for the flashy 'night spots'.

In the autumn of 1980, the newshounds of Fleet Street, television, and half the colour magazines of Europe, once aware that she had been seen with 'HRH' at polo games, horse events, and one or two royal house parties, sensed that this was *the* girl in the Prince of Wales's life, that this was at last the romantic story for which they had been on the look-out for years.

The pretty nineteen-year-old teacher was no Diana the Huntress. She was suddenly, probably as no girl ever had been before, Diana the *hunted*. Day and night, round-the-clock, 'the media' laid siege to that kindergarten school and to the flat which Lady Diana shared with two other girls. Life was made difficult for her; most people would have found it intolerable and would have become understandably short-tempered with

the Press. She couldn't move without a blinding barrage of photographers' flash bulbs exploding around her; reporters rang her doorbells, ran shouting after her car. But her reaction was admirable: she gave nothing away when pestered by reporters' questions for week after week. She remained remarkably courteous; she would laugh and wave to her pursuers. They came to like her very much; they were for the most part astonished at her aplomb as she simply smiled and shook her head in the hail of journalists' questions. She hopped into her Mini, flashed one more smile for them, and sped off. She never gave away the secret that she and the Heir to the Throne were in love.

The secret was well and truly out on the day of that Palace announcement in February, 1981; and from the very hour when the engagement became official, Lady Diana Spencer came under the protective, possessive umbrella of the Royal Family. Gone was private life, with its game of dodging pressmen. She was now, perforce, organized: when she drove out, a plain-clothes police officer drove out too. No longer could she live with her flatmates. She was immediately given the hospitality of – who else? – the Grannie at Clarence House.

July 29, 1981, was fixed as the Wedding date, and the five months between betrothal and marriage were crammed with preparations for the most public royal wedding ever. The Lord Chamberlain's Office buzzed night and day, co-ordinating every detail of procedure with the Palace, the Police, the Army, the authorities of the cities of Westminster and London, and the hierarchy of the Church. St Paul's Cathedral was Prince Charles's own choice for the ceremony.

Presents poured into the Palace and the Queen Mother's

Above *Her Majesty salutes the crowds as she rides in State to her grandson's wedding to Lady Diana Spencer.*

Opposite *The Prince and Princess of Wales drive down Ludgate Hill after their marriage in St Paul's.*

house by the truckload. Such was the public's enthusiasm over the romance that a wideflung Wedding Souvenir industry sprang into being, making and marketing many thousands of commemorative mugs, magazines, books, biscuit tins, T-shirts, goblets of glass and sets of decorated china. Business was brisk. Up and down the country, many a local unemployment problem must have been eased for months.

When the Wedding Day came it proved to be, beyond wildest hopes and dreams, perfect picture-book stuff. A summer of miserable weather miraculously produced hours of golden sunshine to match the glow of the great proceedings and the gladness in all the ranks of spectators. There was never a hitch and never an anxious moment throughout all the pomp and ceremony. It was all very human as well as very handsome. Personal tenderness and a family's genuine happiness touched the emotions of a watching world, and even brought an involuntary catch now and then to the throats of professed republican cynics and blasé professional observers.

It was the media event of our time, watched by a million applauding people on London's streets and, 'live' on television, by 800-million viewers from Yokohama to the Yukon. Broadcasting networks round the globe simply went 'over to London' for the day. Sick of bad news and street riots on their TV sets night after night, the people of Britain and many another country sat happily glued to their screens throughout this one day and took in the pageantry of a real-life royal love story. For a few hours, one felt, evil had been banished and austerity overlooked. Here was Britain doing something it can do supremely well; here was goodness deployed and a nation's morale and pride demonstrably roused. This was not just an Establishment extravaganza. We were all 'sunny side up'. A People's Day.

It was also, of course, very much a Working Day, especially for cohorts of policemen and soldiery and all the unnoticed others whose royal-route vigilance from sewers to rooftops was part of a security operation on a scale not known before.

Left *Prince Charles kisses his bride's hand, a romantic gesture before the crowds demanded a 'real' kiss.*

Below *In the Throne Room of Buckingham Palace, one of the formal portraits of families and bridal attendants.*

Two ladies of style – The Queen Mother and the Princess of Wales leaving Westminster Abbey after a service.

Together again at Royal Braemar, meeting organisers of the Games – the Princess's first public engagement after her marriage.

And Working Day indeed, however joyful, at the Queen Mother's home. For hers was the place from which Prince Charles's bride set out for her wedding. Both she and her sister, Lady Jane, had stayed overnight at Clarence House, which was a keypoint in the whole Operation Marriage.

Down the road in the Royal Mews, coachmen and horses had been grooming and under starter's orders from 5.30 a.m. on July 29. And not long after that hour things started buzzing inside Clarence House. The florist who made the bridal bouquet had been up half the night at her work-table, and she was an early arrival at Queen Elizabeth's household-door, bearing her cascading masterpiece of blooms. Next arrived the hairdresser, make-up girl, a ladies' maid and a lady-in-waiting from the Palace, and the designers of Lady Diana's dress, the young Welsh couple, Elizabeth and David Emanuel. Those two were soon busy, for the bride, very alert but calm, had been up and breakfasted early, and she willingly stood up (at the same time watching the first street scenes on television) whilst 'Liz and David' began to array her in the theatrical dress which was soon to become a world sensation to anybody even faintly fashion-conscious: yards and yards of crushed ivory silk taffeta with its puffed sleeves and huge waves of low, pie-frill neckline. (Lady Diana, in fact, hardly dared to rest for even a moment as the

straightening and crimping of the fabulous frock went on and on – could not sit down, indeed until she was in the Glass Coach; and when in that carriage she arrived at St Paul's Cathedral's West Door the designers had been whisked there from the house and were at the top of the cathedral steps, waiting for her and on their knees again, fussing round to give last-minute adjustments to their creation, the dress which was now adorning a bride who was tiara-crowned above the floating veil and a white train twenty-five feet long.)

Queen Elizabeth The Queen Mother had also been up betimes and in her home was, at an early hour, greeting members of the family, and friends and bridesmaids and pages, who arrived and were able with her to have a private preview of the bride in her finery. Queen Elizabeth was a picture herself in a gown of aquamarine silk; and she was the first of the day's principal figures ceremonially to drive out from the house. In the State processions she rode in one of the many carriages from the Royal Mews. It was open to the sunshine and there she was, with the famous smile and the famous wave for all to see. Beside her rode her then-seventeen-year-old grandson, Prince Edward, this time as a handsome escorting adult. (He was, with Prince Andrew, a 'supporter' of their brother at the marriage service – there is no 'best man' at a royal wedding such as this.)

Opposite *Arriving at the Theatre Royal, Drury Lane – it was Birthday Evening, 1982 – to see 'The Pirates of Penzance'.*

Above *After the show, meeting the stars. The typical welcome of out-stretched arms as Tim Curry and Pamela Stephenson are presented.*

Lady Diana, although she had kept saying to everybody around her in the Queen Mother's bustling house that it was 'the bride's privilege to be late', was in fact ready before starting time and spent several minutes settling herself in the coach at the Clarence House porch before the coachman was given the signal for the 'off'.

Beside her in the coach was her father, John Spencer, eighth Earl – and certainly a man who was one of the heroes of July 29. He was not fully recovered from a severe stroke suffered a few years before, and yet sheer pride and power of endurance carried him, brave and beaming, through hours of standing and walking which might have been a strain on a fit man and must have been physical pain to the Earl. But he was determined to play his part to the full, and he enjoyed every moment of it.

The story of the hours which followed that Wedding Day departure from Clarence House has been written and pictured endlessly. Highlights are indelible in the memory – the deafening cheers in the sanded, garlanded streets as royalty and escorting cavalry made their way in full-dress magnificence to the Cathedral; the immaculate saluting of two brothers in naval uniform as they arrived together: HRH The Bridegroom and Prince Andrew; the multi-coloured sight which the congregation presented as they waited inside the church (it was a remarkable collection of guests, from statesmen and leaders of nations to stand-up comics and variety stage stars who were Prince Charles's friends); the near-miracle by which over two thousand invited people were accommodated in the Cathedral, *plus* huge choirs and orchestras, *plus* Crowned Heads from overseas and our own Royal Family in all its branches, young and old. The Queen, the Duke of Edinburgh, and the Queen Mother were together given pride of place in three ornate chairs.

Slowly pacing through the nave, then, a three-minute walk along a far stretch of red carpet, came bride and father; and behind them the pretty sight of Diana's chosen attendants: five bridesmaids and two pages, most of them young children, but with seventeen-year-old Lady Sarah Armstrong-Jones (Princess Margaret's daughter) in charge. One of the children was a pupil from the kindergarten where the bride had taught: Clementine Hambro, aged five, a great-granddaughter of Sir Winston Churchill. Another, aged ten, was Sarah Jane Gaselee, daughter of Prince Charles's racehorse trainer. One of the pages was Lord Nicholas Windsor, just eleven years old, youngest of the Duke and Duchess of Kent's family.

During the waitings and processions and preliminaries there was ample time – though one seemed not to have eyes enough – to take in the grace and brilliance of the uniforms and hats and

The bride and bridegroom were centrepiece of the inevitable series of appearances on the Palace balcony, waving to an ocean of people massed along The Mall below them. It was then that there came – on cue from the front ranks of the crowd who were shouting 'Go on, Charlie, give her a kiss!' – the royal kiss-in-public which had never happened before and which became instantly famous. The day's other touch of unprecedented informality, hugely enjoyed, was the embellishment of the off-for-the-honeymoon State carriage which later emerged from the Palace, bearing not only the happy couple but clusters of carnival balloons bobbing above them and a piece of cardboard stuck on the back of the landau. The board bore in rough characters the timeless message: 'Just Married!' The words had been scrawled by the bridegroom's exuberant brothers, who had written with a lipstick hastily borrowed from a lady-in-waiting.

Such was the festive day on which the Royal Family was enriched by a very appealing new member.

The press continued to follow the new Princess whenever they could; her official engagements received 'saturation coverage'. Cameramen hopefully haunted the region of the Cotswolds where Highgrove, the first country home of the Prince and Princess is situated, in case the favourite lady should unexpectedly come within lens-shot.

Wedding and honeymoon were still bright in the popular memory when, late in that same year of 1981, official word was given that the Princess was expecting a child. Euphoria blossomed again – with strident commercial echoes: a Royal Baby Souvenir bonanza hummed, whilst some of the left-overs of the *Wedding* Souvenir industry were still going at reduced prices.

More quietly, at Clarence House the Queen Mother looked forward to being a great-grandmother for the third time.

The baby was born on the longest day of 1982's summer: June 21. (Perhaps it seemed the father's longest day too, for the Prince of Wales arrived with his wife early that morning at St Mary's Hospital, Paddington, and was at Her Royal Highness's bedside for sixteen hours, until the birth.) It was a boy! The glad news flashed round the world – *after* a call from the delighted Prince to Queen Elizabeth. *This* great-grandchild was of paramount importance not to be superseded, the Second-in-Line to the Throne. Therefore on some distant day perhaps a king.

All was well at the birth – remarkably well for both the beautiful blue-eyed, seven-pound infant and his healthy young mother, for the Princess of Wales in fact walked out of the hospital on the very next day, bright and smiling, taking turns with the proud father at cradling the child for all the world to see. From the steps of the hospital, she and the Prince drove off to the nursery of their new London apartment, in Kensington Palace, as beaming a pair of parents as has ever been seen.

The christening ceremony was a felicitously timed present for the Queen Mother. It took place on August 4, Her Majesty's eighty-second birthday. So it was a day of double celebration for the family. Queen Elizabeth was still Favourite Royal Person, to

dresses of the prime figures in front rows beneath the cathedral's huge dome. Fashion writers among the journalists, and male connoisseurs too, were generally agreed that one of the most attractive of all the women present was the mother of the bride, the smiling Frances Shand Kydd, beautifully dressed in hyacinth blue.

Attention was rivetted on every detail of the service; even tiny imperfections were relished. When bride and groom exchanged their marriage vows, they were not quite word-perfect: the bride spoke the Prince's names in the wrong order, and he left out the word 'worldly' when saying he would share all his goods with her. The fractional stumbles, far from upsetting anybody, were endearingly human and brought smiles from the family.

The music of the marriage ceremony was as sumptuous as the scene. Every sound and every word spoken was relayed by loud-speakers hung along the streets outside, and many in the crowds joined in the singing and the prayers throughout the service. So all London, and – through satellite broadcasting – half the world, heard the Archbishop, when the ring of Welsh gold had been placed upon the bride's finger, pronounce the couple 'man and wife together'. At which moment Diana Spencer became Princess of Wales.

When the pageantry of the carriage processions flowed back to Buckingham Palace, the streets roared again; and no burst of cheers was louder than the one which greeted the bridegroom's grandmother. There was no doubt that the Queen Mother – who had Prince Andrew with her in the landau this time – was popularly regarded as Fairy Godmother of the day's fairytale romance.

Left *At St Paul's, the Prince of Wales and his bride had walked in procession past the Royal Family before traversing the Nave to the West Door.*

Below *Balcony scene, July 29, 1981, after the return from St Paul's. The bridal couple are framed by the Queen Mother and Prince Philip on one side and by the Queen and Prince Charles's two 'Supporters', his brothers Prince Edward and Prince Andrew, on the other. Small pages and bridesmaids get a good look-in.*

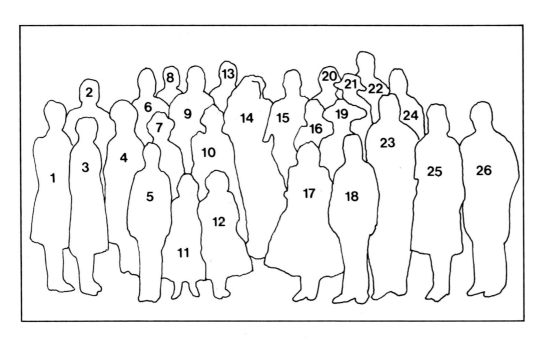

Pages 132 and 133. *Picture for the Royal Album. The full family group posed for the camera in Buckingham Palace on the Great Wedding Day of July 1981. Present are: 1. Princess Anne; 2. Captain Mark Phillips; 3. Princess Margaret; 4. Queen Elizabeth The Queen Mother; 5. Edward van Cutsem; 6. Prince Andrew; 7. The Queen; 8. Viscount Linley; 9. Prince Philip; 10. India Hicks; 11. Clementine Hambro; 12. Catherine Cameron; 13. Prince Edward; 14. The Princess of Wales; 15. The Prince of Wales; 16. Lady Sarah Armstrong-Jones; 17. Sarah Jane Gaselee; 18. Lord Nicholas Windsor; 19. the Hon. Mrs. Frances Shand Kydd; 20. Ruth, Lady Fermoy; 21. Lady Jane Fellowes; 22. Viscount Althorp; 23. Earl Spencer; 24. Mr Robert Fellowes; 25. Lady Sarah McCorquodale; 26. Mr. Neil McCorquodale.*

judge by the behaviour of the singing and cheering hundreds who gathered from an early hour that morning outside her home, and were rewarded when, light-footed and radiant as ever, she came walking out from the Clarence House gates to receive spontaneous gifts of posies and sweets from children who had popped out, like pips from an orange, from the straining crowd barriers. Then Her Majesty drove along to the baptismal service held in the handsome Music Room of Buckingham Palace which has often served as a chapel for royal christenings.

Prince William Arthur Philip Louis was the name given to baby. During the half-hour service, conducted by the Archbishop of Canterbury, the infant prince behaved impeccably. But it was a different story in the next room afterwards. A long session for the taking of group photographs, family and godparents all round, and small William always in the middle, proved to much for the now-hungry bairn. Lovely though he looked in the famous lace christening robe handed down from Queen Victoria's days, he was not comfortable and not content any longer. He was bored with posing and bothered by the bright lamps. Soon he was howling inconsolably as he was held in turn by grandmother and great-grandmother; and the loud cries did not stop until his mother again took him in her arms and popped her little finger into his mouth. That did the trick. William of Wales sucked the finger with mighty gusto and manifest hope.

The Queen Mother had regarded her tiny descendant's hullabaloo with equanimity. 'Quite right,' she said. 'He's wanting lunch; he's made his first public speech; and he's got good lungs.' It was all part of a birthday to cherish.

Above *One-day old, in his mother's arms, the royal baby goes home to Kensington Palace from the Paddington hospital. The Princess's shy smile enchanted the waiting crowds.*

Opposite *August 4, 1982, was a date of double celebration. It was the Queen Mother's Eighty-second birthday and was chosen as the day of the Christening of her great-grandson, Prince William, then little more than six weeks old. The ceremony took place at the Palace, where this picture of four generations was taken. The infant Second-in-Line was comforted only by sucking the little finger of his mother, the Princess of Wales.*

Right *In a great-grandmother's arms this time – Prince William voices his views.*

CHAPTER 9

Homes—and Horses

GRACIOUS CENTRE of many a special occasion though she is, the Queen Mother's existence is not just a fabric of publicised high days and holidays. She is sustained in her celebrations and official duties by her lesser-known activities 'off stage', by being at ease with relatives and friends, by her hobbies and recreations, by her absorbing homes and gardens, and by deep-rooted affection for animals – a love which takes several forms. She is the same radiant human being, at home or away. But her private life is a foundation of her public joy.

Firstly, she is a gardener *par excellence*. It is in her blood. Not

Opposite *Windsor Castle, noblest of royal residences, home of kings for nine centuries.*

Below *At Chelsea Flower Show with Lord Aberconway (left), President of the RHS, admiring a rose named after his wife, Ann Aberconway.*

that she fiddles with flower-arrangements or fusses round potting sheds – though she still has skill with vase and trowel. Her delight is in the management of her own acres, her feeling for layout and landscape, window-boxes too. Almost all the gardens of the royal houses in London, Windsor, Norfolk's Sandringham and Scotland's Deeside and Mey have been within her care at one time or another. She has had a hand in the development of all of them.

She is in the tradition of a long line of British kings and queens who have been makers of lovely homes and fine gardens. Henry VIII inspired the splendid intricacies of Hampton Court; Charles II brought the new French planning which first beautified Windsor and St James's; William and Mary imported the formal glories of Dutch gardens into Kensington and Hampton too; and royal encouragement spurred the Georgian and Victorian enterprises which created the Royal

Botanic Gardens, Kew, one of the most famous and publicly visited of the world's great gardens. She retains pride in Buckingham Palace where, as the thousands of people who have been to royal garden parties know, there are forty-five private acres of horticulturist's delight behind the Nash building and its public face, the over-photographed Victorian east front. Windsor Castle has widespread estates. A royal home and fortress for over nine hundred years, its spacious parklands and innumerable gardens laid out under the old walls and towers, as well as the tightly managed Windsor farms and vegetable acres, were known in considerable detail by King George VI and Queen Elizabeth. So it was also with that other Royal Palace which stands in the Scottish capital, Edinburgh: Holyroodhouse, with its cunning ha-ha wall and those giant cultivated thistles which in lines of sentinel tubs are as straight and regimented as the ranks of the bodyguard Royal Company of Archers who parade in the grounds when the Royal Family are in residence.

Holyrood is official, a State palace; but the other Scottish house, Balmoral, is private property, the loved holiday hideout deep in Aberdeenshire's invigorating mountains and forests. The castle is a fine baronial pile constructed in the middle of last century by the virtuous Victoria and her virtuoso Consort when they became obsessed with the Highlands and splendoured their castle's rooms with a rash of clan tartans. The old atmosphere has not gone: Victoria would still be at home there. But the

natural setting of Balmoral is its chief joy. Above the river and the great house rise the wild moors and steep slopes of pine and heather, the uninhabited miles of deer forest studded by tarns. It is one of the largest areas of natural woodland in all the realm.

But Royal Deeside is not all Balmoral. There is more to it than the castle, certainly from the Queen Mother's point of view. For she has there her own Highland home: Birkhall, a dower house of the castle. It stands beside the River Muick about eight miles from the great *Schloss* which Prince Albert built, and not far from Ballater. Birkhall is a plain, white-walled and relatively small Queen Anne house, to which Her Majesty has added new wings, furnished under her tasteful supervision. It is lower in altitude and in warmer air than Balmoral and it has an attractive garden sloping down to the stream. Much of the garden was planned by the Queen and King George VI when they first lived in the house as Duke and Duchess of York in George V's time – they were in fact staying in the house in 1936 when the Abdication crisis was coming to a head and Edward VIII and Mrs Simpson were holding incongruous parties up at the castle.

Birkhall is a house of happiness, unpretentious and informal. It is enjoyed by many members of the Family, especially when the Queen Mother is in residence up there in the autumn, usually after a short stay at Mey. She likes to entertain her friends – her grandchildren and *their* friends among them – out of doors and in her own alfresco style as well as a little more cosily indoors. She will still play picnic leader and organizer,

Opposite *The gardens at Royal Lodge were laid out by King George and Queen Elizabeth with much of the work being done by their own hands; week-end guests and visitors were often persuaded to help. Even flagstones such as these were royally laid.*

Above *Behind the terrace can be seen the windows of the Saloon, a magnificently proportioned room some fifty feet long, twenty feet wide and thirty feet high.*

Right *Every part of the terrace at Royal Lodge commands fine views of the gardens and their huge old cedar trees.*

though striding the hills a shade more gently nowadays. Through the years, very much in the footsteps of Victoria, she and her parties have explored remote Loch Muick and the Lochnagar country, with dogs and guns, cold mist and rain notwithstanding.

She still fishes the Dee. This is a sport at which Her Majesty has been long accomplished. She has taught it to all her grandsons and their contemporaries (though Prince Charles is probably the only one who can tie a fly as well as she can).

Today there stands on the Balmoral estate, in a very attractive and romantic spot beside the river and not very far from the South Dee side-road, a recent but well loved little building, simple and perhaps not much more than a large hut. This is the Log Cabin, already well established as a small fishing rendezvous and picnic spot for the Queen Mother, her family and friends, her summer-and-autumn visitors, and fortunate members of her Household. It is just logs and bare wood, with two verandas, one looking across the river and the other facing downstream. Rods and tackle and haversacks may be found strewn around it during the season, the time when the track to the hut is quite often busy with the comings and goings of royal Daimler or Land Rover.

The Cabin is no architectural gem; but in its way is a little treasure-house. For it was an eightieth birthday present to Queen Elizabeth from members of her family and friends. It has been furnished partly by a variety of birthday gifts from her regiments and from some organisations of which she is patron. The pine tables, sideboard and chairs were a particularly liked gift from the Cavalry Regiments of which Her Majesty is Colonel-in-Chief or Honorary Colonel. The Knights of the Garter and the Knights of the Thistle each gave a wicker armchair, the cushions of the one chair covered in Garter-blue and those of the other in Thistle-green.

The place can be made thoroughly warm by lighting the excellent wood-burning stove. So, even in wet and cold weather, to this Cabin the royal owner happily and cosily goes on every possible day – even sometimes for a candle-lit evening – when she is in residence at Birkhall. The site is agreeable in almost any weather, and is near one of Queen Elizabeth's favourite fishing pools, Polveir. It is a joy simply to be there, to take in the scenery, and to enjoy picnics either indoors, or on a veranda, or outside on the grass.

Their holiday homes in Aberdeenshire give the Royal Family welcome weeks each year to relax and rest, out of the limelight. Their church attendances for Sunday morning service – at Crathie when they are in Scotland and at Sandringham's little parish church when in Norfolk – have traditionally been almost the only occasions when it has been possible for the general public to catch a glimpse of them.

But the place of worship to which the family go on many Sundays of every year is one which is not generally seen at all. For it is situated almost alongside the Queen Mother's week-end home near London, Royal Lodge, in the private part of Windsor Great Park. This interesting little church was begun by George IV, when at the height of his mania for ordering buildings to be constructed or altered. Much later, Queen Victoria gave the church a homely look, with just a touch of a Scottish village kirk; and she had flowering trees and rose-covered fences set around it.

Queen Elizabeth walks along from the Lodge for morning

Left *One of a pair of magnificent cedars as seen from the terrace. These with other trees at the front of the Royal Lodge, are said to have marked the boundaries of the original house before the reign of George IV.*

Opposite, top *The statue, Charity, is a copy of an original standing at St Paul's Walden Bury, made by Sir Henry Cheere (1703–81). At Royal Lodge this replica has been set most carefully at a high point in the gardens, leading down to the Lodge through a beautiful display of rhododendrons and azaleas, which are at their best in late spring.*

Opposite, bottom *Pets and family on the lawn at the Royal Lodge, Windsor, in 1936.*

service at this Royal Chapel of All Saints, whilst the Queen and Prince Philip and their family and friends drive up through the Great Park from Windsor Castle. (They attend service in the Castle's own magnificent St George's Chapel only on special occasions.)

Once inside the church-in-the-park, the Royal Family occupy a special stall in the chancel out of sight of the rest of the congregation, which is made up mainly of tenant families, estate workers and others who have houses on the Windsor lands. Although this royal stall is tucked away, King George VI liked to have a sight of the rest of the pews, so he had a cut made in one of the pillars of the chancel arch. With the aid of this, when he leaned forward he was able to see who was present – and who not! – in the rows of worshippers. His widow, the Queen Mother, nowadays sits in his seat – and *she* has the habit of peeping round the pillar.

The Royal Lodge, Windsor, of all the homes in which she regularly lives, is Queen Elizabeth's first love. The house stands in the same relation to Windsor Castle as Birkhall does to grand Balmoral. But, close to London as it is, and because of its comfort and special associations, Her Majesty spends a great deal more time there than at any other out-of-town house. Strictly and legally, the Lodge belongs to the reigning Sovereign, as Windsor Castle does, but it has for long been the Queen Mother's own place. And it is quite private, never seen by the public although it lies close by the south-eastern edge of the Great Park, near to Englefield Green and half way between the Castle and Virginia Water. Long ago Queen Elizabeth took Royal Lodge to her heart, and it has her mark upon it. No wonder: she has known it intimately for half a century, and for most of that span has been

its contented occupant. Its grounds and gardens are essentially a little country world shaped by herself and the late King. Working in its woodlands, they spent many of the happiest times of their lives together.

They first saw the Lodge in 1931 when, as Duke and Duchess of York, they were driven over from the Castle by the old King to have a look around what was then – although it was one of the several specially built and maintained old hunting lodges of Windsor's royal estates – a neglected and dilapidated house with an overgrown thirty-acre wilderness around it. It had been virtually unoccupied for a hundred years. Daunting jungle though the Lodge and its grounds seemed, the Duke and Duchess nevertheless eagerly accepted when George V offered them the place as a grace-and-favour residence. Their only house then was the London one in Piccadilly, and they leaped at the chance of having a quiet country home. (It was long before Heathrow Airport's screaming monsters of the jet-ridden sky made Windsor one of the noisiest places in England.) Especially, they wanted the joy of making a woodland garden.

The Duchess, no less than the Duke (and George VI had a passion and a real talent for landscape gardening), saw the possibilities in the Lodge from the outset. Her gardening enthusiasm no doubt overwhelmed any small displeasure which the Scottish Jacobite in her might have felt at the prospect of going to live in a house which had once been in the hands of 'Butcher' Cumberland, the victor of tragic Culloden! For the Lodge had a chequered history.

The first house on the site, built in the eighteenth century, was at one time lived in by Thomas Sandby, who was quite a painter in his own right though not so famous as his artist brother, Paul. Both men drew and painted the house and its surroundings many times. Thomas Sandby had been secretary and deputy to the notorious Duke of Cumberland, third son of George II, when, after Cumberland's cruel work as a British general in the Highlands, he was made Ranger of Windsor Great Park and began to rebuild the Lodge for himself. The Prince Regent who became George IV lived at the house late in his life whilst his vast remodelling of Windsor Castle and other Windsor lodges was going on. Then he decided that this Royal Lodge should itself be rebuilt – typically, it was to be on a gradiose scale, part Nash and part Wyatville – but the work was never finished. The next monarch, the impoverished William IV, tried to live there but then had most of the place pulled down. Little other than the one big room of the house, the Saloon, remained when Victoria was on the Throne; after her death still more additions to this main feature were made, with a lamentable mixing of architectural styles.

Queen Elizabeth loved the Lodge from the start. In those early Thirties when she was Duchess of York she worked hard, for here was a garden of her very own. Whilst the house itself was being made habitable, she and her husband were busy planning paths and rides, lawns and vistas, and beginning the clearance of accumulations of undergrowth, untouched for years, which encompassed the building. She worked knowledgeably, for she had been a gardener since childhood. She had learned her skills from her mother, Lady Strathmore, an acknowledged expert,

Opposite In May 1954 with Princess Margaret at the Chelsea Flower Show, held in the grounds of the Royal Hospital.

Left Always having had a great interest in horses, the Queen Mother is a regular visitor to Badminton for the Three-Day Event. Among those with her here are her host, the Duke of Beaufort, several members of the Royal Family, and some friends.

Below At Royal Ascot in 1976. Behind the Queen Mother is Her Majesty the Queen. Also seen in the photograph are Princess Margaret, the Marquess of Abergavenny (with the umbrella), and to his left Lord Porchester. On the Queen's left is Major W. H. (Dick) Hern.

phenomenally green-fingered, and from the gardens she herself had made as a small girl at Glamis and St Paul's Walden Bury.

Her Majesty always maintains, however, that at Royal Lodge she was *assistant* gardener and that the real architect of the fine gardens there was her husband. Certainly when King George VI, as Duke of York, was first given the Lodge he flung himself with infectious zest into the Herculean task of clearing the wild growths that were throttling the woodlands, revelling in the creation of winding paths and clean rides in the grounds around the house.

The royal work parties themselves must have made an amusing picture in those days. Whenever possible on Saturdays and Sundays the Duke and Duchess would go down to the Lodge, taking a cold lunch, and spend the weekend in bush-clearing, hacking through thickets, making great bonfires of old wood as they lopped trees, put in new plants and laid the foundations of lawns and green avenues. Battle orders were issued by the Duke, old clothes were put on, axes and saws and pruning bills were distributed, and all hands were pressed into service.

The Queen Mother recalls afternoons when vistors, perhaps calling for tea, were at once conscripted to join the gangs in which, side by side and indistinguishable one from the other, there worked princess and secretary, duke and valet, equerry and chauffeur, butler and policeman, all covered in dirt and twigs as they hacked and crawled through the tangled thickets together. One Saturday a huge Guards officer became part of the gang. Wanting to get used to wearing his black bearskin hat – it was a new one and would have to be worn at a full-dress parade the following week – he put it on whilst acting as wheel-

Opposite, top *With Princess Anne, the Duke of Kent and Lord Snowdon in an open landau at Ascot in 1973.*

Opposite, bottom *Her Majesty arriving with Princess Margaret at the Royal Opera House to attend a Silver Jubilee Gala Performance.*

Above *Connoisseur of fragrance at the 1956 Chelsea Show.*

Right *At Villa d'Este in Tivoli during her visit to Italy in 1959.*

barrow labourer for the Duke. As the afternoon became hotter
and hotter he toiled on, stripped himself to the waist, covered his
middle with nothing but an old pair of khaki shorts, but kept his
towering furry headgear strapped to his head.

It was one of the joys of George VI's life that gardening
expertise came easily to him. He was never showy with his
garden knowledge, but the minutiae of it appealed to his
meticulous and tidy mind. He became a devotee of flower shows,
increasingly erudite when it came to naming plants. To friends
he sometimes wrote entertaining letters composed almost
entirely of the dog-latin terms used by shrub specialists.

In wartime the visits to the Lodge were of necessity fewer (the
1939 underground air-raid shelters are still there at the back of
the house, incidentally). When peace came again in the years
after 1945 they once more took the Lodge into their personal
care and occupation. So, gradually over the years, the grounds
became what they are today, tended and cultivated, a joy in
their contrived informality. It was under the hands of that royal
husband and wife, and later to the solace and pleasure of Queen
Elizabeth as Queen Mother, that those lovely green acres of the
Lodge became a lived-with, cared-for joy. There are small
patches of more conventional garden at the Lodge too. They are
near to the house, and are equally in Queen Elizabeth's care:
sunken garden, herbaceous borders, the rosemary and the
hyacinths, the tall *Magnolia grandiflora* at the western end of the
terrace, the specially liked borders of lavender on the east
terrace, the beds of roses called Elizabeth of Glamis, and the
lemon-scented verbena which Her Majesty always touches as
she comes into the back porch which guards the main door.

The Royal Lodge today is a pleasant, pink-washed country
house, yet not pretentious and not a great mansion. Without its
rural setting it might be unremarkable. Without the tasteful,
comfortable way in which the Queen Mother has furnished the
house, making it a bright and welcoming home, it might have
been unremarkable within. But it certainly is not.

The main room is still the Saloon, which happily possesses the
proportions which Prinny's builder gave to it: fifty feet long,
twenty wide and thirty high (and, incidentally, George IV is
still there, looking grand in the portrait by Sir Thomas
Lawrence which hangs above the fireplace). Her Majesty has
made it beautifully homely, as she has the adjoining Octagon
Room and the house's modern additions upstairs. Her own
favourite writing desk is beside a French window of the Octagon
Room: sitting there, she has only to turn her head to see the herb
garden and the flower beds a few feet away.

But no visitor would deny that the Saloon is the heart and the
showpiece of the house. Its five great windows all in a row lead to
the wide terrace and the enchanting views of spreading lawns
and woodlands, the brilliant aprons of natural grass and wide
green avenues all bordered by azaleas and camelias, the mass
upon mass of rhododendrons of many varieties, the carefully
contrived bushes, and the two tremendous old cedar trees not far
from the terrace – the whole scene is a joy.

Royal Lodge, in short, is the Queen Mother's greatly loved
retreat. But, busy person as she is, much time has to be spent at
her London home and headquarters. Clarence House – as
already told – is historic, but externally is not anything like so
notable as it is when you go inside. Within the place, you at once
begin to see another facet of Her Majesty's life and character:
she is an art collector – and, as in everything else, of individual
taste. She inherited a number of fine large pictures when she
went to live in the house thirty years ago. Former kings and

princes look down from the walls: paintings by Lely, Allan Ramsay and the Schools of Beechey and Hoppner.

But Queen Elizabeth's own acquisitions are more interesting. In fact, ever since her years as Queen Consort, she has brought back a discerning royal patronage of artists which had lapsed since the time of Victoria's Albert. She has a sound purchasing judgement and an instinctive pleasure in a variety of appealing paintings. Lively taste is reflected also in the china and silver and period furniture. They embellish, but do not overpower the rooms – which are cosy and elegant at the same time.

It is fascinating, I think, to see all the indexes of her character, in face and dress, which are to be found in the many likenesses of herself on the crowded walls of Clarence House and elsewhere. These of course are paintings on canvas, but there are classic photographs too. Camera artists like Cecil Beaton, Marcus Adams, Tony Snowdon, Norman Parkinson and Patrick Lichfield, photographers of royalty, have left lasting reminders of the fact that the present is as much an Age of Photography as of painting. Portraits are important here because, more often than not, they immediately give more reality to our ideas and

Above *Accepting a painting while visiting the Mission of the Dutch Reformed Church at Morgenster, near Fort Victoria, in July, 1953, during her tour of Southern Rhodesia.*

Right *Her Majesty discusses with the art master a mural designed by two senior students, when she opened the new buildings of the Archbishop Tenison School, Croydon, in November 1959.*

memories of Queen Elizabeth's sweetness and verve than a whole handful of biographies – just as in earlier reigns the Holbein and Van Dyck pictures made their viewers feel, and make us feel to this day, the aristocratic strength of Henry VIII, for instance, and the essence of cavalier romanticism that was in the first King Charles.

Sittings for artists (and for other professionals too, such as dressmakers, for that matter) are one of the inescapable duties of Royalty, and never a week passes without some request arriving at Clarence House from a regiment, a municipality, City company or overseas nation, for authority to commission a portrait.

Since the Eightieth Birthday, the number of sittings seem to have been greater than ever. They cannot of course be long sessions: painters need to have a fast brush. But this lady is a favourite sitter. She does not bother an artist with questions or instructions on how she would like the finished product to look; and she keeps quite still when asked to do so though her conversation goes on flowing freely enough!

Her Majesty owns one portrait herself which is unusual, to say the least, and has a bizarre history. It is an Augustus John, unfinished. It shows a figure facing straight at the painter. The evening gown is full and impressive; but as to the face, it is strangely odd and hardly the Queen's. The sittings for this portrait took place in Buckingham Palace during the first few months of the war, when the sitter was Queen Consort. John, himself so boldly Bohemian and picturesque a person, was temperamental, doubtful, and apparently shy when the dates for the sittings approached; and more than once he failed to arrive. He confessed to being as enchanted as everyone else when he did turn up, but it was clear to the royal Household that he was tense and dissatisfied. Sittings were a struggle and the picture a mess. However, when a bottle of brandy was placed in the cupboard where the artist kept his painting gear and a string quartet was brought in to play in the anteroom, Augustus John became more relaxed.

But Hitler interrupted the painting: sittings were broken off when the Blitz began. Then, in 1942, when London was quieter but battered by the air-raid bombs, the Queen sent a message to the artist to say that she would be willing for the work to be completed. She would go to his studio, she said, 'if you have any windows, for we have none here in Buckingham Palace, and it is too dark and dusty to paint anyway.' But John had shut the canvas away. Years later, in 1961, the year of the artist's death, a foraging art dealer found the portrait, deep in dust and spiders, in the cellars beneath John's studio; and some time afterwards it was presented to the Queen Mother for her collection. Today it hangs, evidently liked by Her Majesty but looking enigmatically crude and clearly uncompleted, over the mantelpiece in the garden room at Clarence House. It has come home, a curio, after forty years.

By royal standards, the art world would probably call Queen Elizabeth's taste as a buyer of paintings advanced, independent and more personal than most, sometimes capricious, but with a real feel for quality. She is particularly fond of artists of modern periods; in Clarence House you may find Sickerts, Wilson Steers, a Sidney Nolan, an Ethel Walker, a couple of Sorine portraits, one of Paul Nash's *Landscapes of the Vernal Equinox*, Simon Elwes studies of George VI and others, as well as various royal family portraits, wide-ranging in size and style, painted during the last one hundred years. There is a notable John Singer Sargent of Queen Elizabeth herself in 1923, the year of her marriage, and two 1931 de Laszlos of herself and her husband. There is Sisley's *The Seine near St Cloud*.

Right *In the City Hall Museum during her visit to Rome in 1959, the Queen Mother listens attentively as the Capitoline Wolf Sculpture and the Romulus-and-Remus legend are explained.*

Opposite *The Lady Elizabeth on 'Bobs', her favourite pony – a cherished family album picture.*

The strong sense of family – her own family – is illustrated. Year after year Her Majesty has bought from salerooms a goodly number of pictures and other possessions which were the property of her Bowes and Lyon forbears. Among them are impressive horse pictures. A large Hoppner of the tenth Earl of Strathmore with his charger catches the eye. Much smaller is a watercolour by Herring of Thomas Lyon-Bowes, the twelfth Earl who was the Queen Mother's great-uncle. He is jockey-mounted and wearing his racing colours. There are echoes too of that John Bowes of Streatlam Castle in County Durham who had four Derby winners.

Among many other reminders of racing which are to be seen in Clarence House are the collections of silver which include, as well as fine period pieces and gifts that are mementos of years of royal travel and State occasions, trophies of Her Majesty's own distinguished career as a leading racehorse breeder. And among the abundance of English cups on display there is a prize replica from the Northern Realm – the Lanark Bell, won by George VI with Kingstone in 1946, the year after the war. The annual race for this Bell is of great age, and certainly of particular appeal to a Scottish Queen. The race is on record as having been run in the middle of the seventeenth century, and it is believed to have been founded four hundred years before then, by none other than King William the Lion of Scotland, surely one of the Queen Mother's ancestors.

The Royal Family's enthusiasm for riding and racing is proverbial, and Queen Elizabeth herself comes from a family which knew all about the breeding and training of horses. Her own years as a racehorse owner began soon after she had become King George VI's Queen. The late Lord Mildmay of Fleet started it in 1949 when at an Ascot Week dinner party he talked about the excitements of riding 'over the sticks'. Anthony Mildmay was a superb and very popular amateur rider – old hands still remember the crowds' roaring of 'Come on, Lordy!' as time after time he stormed home to win – and his enthusiasm for steeplechasing fired Her Majesty. Her interest grew, and as Queen Mother she became a keen and acutely knowledgeable owner, reaching a heyday in the seasons between 1968 and 1971, by which time she was one of the most successful, certainly the most loved, owners in National Hunt history. A ripple of pleasure has always gone round a course when the word has been passed among trainers, jockeys and stable lads: 'The Queen Mum's here!' She has always preferred the winter game to the Flat, and it is in no small measure due to her that steeplechasing has become a national sport.

Year after year, Major Peter Cazalet, a great friend, trained the horses for her at his lovely home, Fairlawne in West Kent. His death in 1973 came as much more than the loss of a trainer of 'chasers. With Her Majesty he had been at the heart of the great post-war surge of organized riding-over-fences; and for the royal owner he symbolised an era. But nothing stopped the Queen Mother racing; and since the Fairlawne days all her horses have been in the expert charge of Fulke Walwyn at Lambourn.

Looking back, the horse which royal owner and general public will never forget was the one which bore the name of Devon Loch. He provided a heartbreaking drama at the 1956

Above, left *King George VI and Queen Elizabeth follow the 1937 Grand National through their glasses.*

Above, right *At Sandown Park in March 1954 Lieutenant Colonel Blacker bows to the Queen Mother, after she had presented the Grand Military Gold Cup to him for winning the race on Pointsman.*

Left *In June 1953 the Queen, with the late Duke of Norfolk, walks to the paddock after the Queen's horse, Choirboy, had won the Royal Hunt Cup at Ascot. Queen Elizabeth The Queen Mother, Princess Margaret, the Princess Royal and the Duchess of Gloucester follow.*

Right *Devon Loch, owned by Her Majesty, won the Sandown Handicap Steeplechase in 1955. The Queen Mother joins trainer Peter Cazalet and jockey Dick Francis in the unsaddling enclosure. It was the year before the horse's sensational Grand National collapse.*

Right *In September 1973 the Queen Mother cuts the tape and declares open the new stand and enclosure at Sandown Park racecourse.*

Grand National. His jockey was Dick Francis (since then a highly prolific and widely read writer of racecourse novels), and throughout the gruelling race he had ridden marvellously. Then, when only fifty yards from the winning-post and six lengths ahead of every remaining runner, the unbelievable happened: the crowds were yelling joy at a royal victory which seemed an absolute certainty when suddenly, inexplicably, Devon Loch collapsed flat-out on the turf. He couldn't at once get up on his feet; and Francis stood helpless beside his mount, in tears. Anyone else but the Queen Mother would have been in

tears too. But no. Though the cup of triumph had been dashed from her lips, she was self-controlled as ever, and her first thought was to go down from the royal box to console the stricken jockey and congratulate the surprised winner. All she said publicly was: 'Well, that's racing.'

And she still has her finger on the pulse of the racing world. Though she does not herself bet (and never has done), 'the Blower' has long been installed in Clarence House. Through its telephone lines comes all the information on runners, state of the going, and starting prices, jockeys and everything else, just as in

Left *Royal encouragement before the start of a point-to-point. With Her Majesty is the Duke of Beaufort, then Master of the Horse in the Sovereign's Household.*

Below *Excitement in the Royal Box as Lester Piggott on The Minstrel wins the 1977 Derby. (From the left) The Queen Mother, the Duke of Kent, Princess Alexandra, the Hon. Angus Ogilvy and the Duchess of Kent.*

Opposite *August 1, 1979. A proud day for Her Majesty and the South-East coast as, now Lord Warden and Admiral of the Cinque Ports, she drives in procession from Dover Castle, whose Constable she became on the same historic day.*

Left *Gala smiles match the gala ballet staged at Covent Garden on the evening of Queen Elizabeth's Eightieth Birthday. She took her whole family to the Opera House. Here, in the Royal Box, Princess Margaret is beside her mother.*

Below *On the day of the Eightieth Birthday Thanksgiving Service, the Queen Mother, back at the Palace, gathered her six grandchildren about her for this photograph. Standing, from the left, are Viscount Linley, Prince Andrew, the Prince of Wales and Prince Edward. On Her Majesty's left is Princess Anne, and Lady Sarah Armstrong-Jones sits at her other side.*

Opposite *Precious transfer. The Prince and Princess of Wales on the steps of St Mary's Hospital, Paddington, London, with their infant son born only the day before, June 21, 1982.*

Opposite *The Lord Mayor of London escorts the Queen Mother up the steps of St Paul's for the great Birthday Service of 1980. Prince Charles is in attendance.*

a thousand betting-shops. And the Sandown, Kempton, Cheltenham and other meetings often come to view at a flick of one of the house's television sets. But it is best to have it all at first hand of course; and Her Majesty goes racing whenever she can. Her interest remains unimpaired. Few owners in the land can come anywhere near matching her knowledge and experience, her love of horses and her care for the good name of the sport she follows.

Through the years she has owned some 350 winners. Her memory for the facts as well as the sheer thrills behind that record is remarkably full and accurate, even without recourse to the private racing notebooks of that great enthusiast who serves her, Sir Martin Gilliat, Private Secretary to the Queen Mother for well over a quarter of a century and doyen now of all the senior members of the royal households. Nowadays Her Majesty's scale of operations as an owner of 'chasers is much more modest than it used to be. Unusually there are about seven horses in training at Lambourn, compared with fifteen or so in the great days gone by at Fairlawne, when there would be a score of winners in a season. Six winners is a more likely figure now; and of course the sport has become much more competitive. Not for some time have there been among her horses such well established characters as – to mention only three of many outstanding performers – The Rip, Double Star and Devon Loch. But the stables are frequently visited and detailed plans are worked out, under the royal eye, for every one of her horses. In addition to the mounts in training, there are around six broodmares and some foals at Sandringham and nearby Wolferton, whence many of the young entries stem.

Each of Queen Elizabeth's horses, when its racing days are over, is carefully placed by its owner to be sure that it goes to a good home; and Her Majesty either visits them or makes a point of keeping in touch with their well-being. She does not *sell* her horses. It would be like selling a friend.

And so it is also with dogs: to her, they are more than pets or playthings. This is characteristic of all the Royal Family. Animal-lovers is a barely adequate term for them. In their houses and grounds, it seems, there are dogs everywhere. House dogs, gun dogs, beautiful Labradors and various others. To young and old they are a natural part of the family.

For the past fifty years it is the stumpy little smooth-coated Welsh corgis which have dominated the *ménages* – one almost wrote menageries – of the Family. And it was Queen Elizabeth, whilst she was Duchess of York, who introduced this short-tailed Pembroke breed. Her daughter, a small Princess Elizabeth, had seen a friend's corgi pup and had fallen in love with it; and she

Above *The Queen Mother studies Lester Piggott riding The Minstrel just before he went to his superb Jubilee Derby victory in 1977.*

Below *Fishing in the River Dee, with ghillie in attendance. Queen Elizabeth's angling expertise is something she still possesses; she has taught all her grandsons the fisherman's art.*

Opposite *The Queen Mother is an avid fisherman, at home or away. Here, she is after lake trout in New Zealand during her 1966 tour.*

Above *One of the royal corgis demands attention from his mistress. The Queen Mother was attending a reception at St James's Palace in December 1972.*

and the Duke managed to buy Elizabeth a similar one. From that moment the years of faithful corgi-owning began. The breed was little known then, in 1933, when that first of the royal line of dogs – called Dookie, a contraction of 'the Duke of York's puppy' – arrived at 145 Piccadilly, but since then there have been whole generations of corgis.

The Queen Mother has remained faithful to the breed. The current pair of little dogs are veterans named Geordie and Blackie, and they have for years been followers at her heels or forerunners wherever she moves. They are loved companions, personally fed by their mistress whenever that is possible; but they are not drooled over. The royal lady is quite aware that, though attractive and intelligent, these small animals are of a stock which can at times betray uncertain temper and disagreeable teeth. Geordie may well roll over to be tickled, even by a stranger. But not Blackie. He is the one to beware of.

He has sometimes given cause for guests, sentries, servants, and sundry other humans privately to describe the likes of *that* dog as snappy little beasts.

Regular members of Her Majesty's Household, though occasionally they may have nursed a bite-scarred ankle or finger, do not take the menace too seriously; and indeed there is cherished in Clarence House a cutting of a large newspaper headline, printed after a footman allegedly suffered a slight abrasion in the course of his duties: 'ROYAL CORGI STRIKES AGAIN!'

It would be difficult to envisage Queen Elizabeth *without* her dogs. They have become part of her domestic image – part of her whole family's image – in the public mind. Well she knows it. She is unlikely to have been offended, very likely to have been tickled, when a comedian, parodying Gershwin, once suggested a royal opera to be called 'Corgi and Bess'.

CHAPTER 10

Herself and the Family

THE LIFE of this Royal Lady is so rich in years that she must need recourse to her diaries not only to keep track of recurring public engagements, but also the advents and anniversaries of her own people, the family she crowns as a marvellous, much-loved matriarch.

Queen Elizabeth warms increasingly now to old Scottish friends and kinsfolk: the Bowes-Lyons, the Elphinstones, the descendants of the Strathmore house from which she came. However, it is her other kin, the large Royal Family, whom she naturally and most often sees – the princes and princesses and royal dukes and duchesses, and *their* children, the Gloucester and Kent great-nephews and great-nieces and cousins in plenty. The family tree has healthily spread, branch from branch, out of a main stem strong and tall; and there are eight decades between the star sprig, baby Prince William of Wales, and his great-grandmother.

Her Majesty's direct line, her daughters and their own young, are of course closest to her heart; and their fondness and respect for *her* needs no embroidering. But she also much enjoys being a centre of affection to all the others of very varied ages, those who descend from her late husband's brothers. The wide web of the Windsor generations today make a genealogist's joy. The family circle has expanded enough to tempt comparison with the prolific Victorian spread.

For twenty years before *the* Great Wedding of 1981 – its splendour still so fresh that memory of earlier lovely marriages may have faded a little – the Queen Mother beamed on wedding after wedding, birth after birth. One of the marriages gave a special pleasure to her. It was the 1963 event, when the universally popular Princess Alexandra of Kent became the Honourable Mrs Angus Ogilvy. The bridegroom was a son of the twelfth Earl of Airlie, for many years Her Majesty's Lord Chamberlain, and the Airlie family had a long record of service to and close friendship with royalty. Angus proposed to the Princess during one of the Queen Mother's house parties at Birkhall, and the house was lent for the honeymoon. The marriage also appealed to the Queen Mother's sense of history: it linked her family, the Strathmores, and the great patrician Airlie family even more closely than geography had done through the centuries. (Glamis and the Airlies' castle at Kirriemuir are neighbours.)

Opposite *A Queen for all weathers, happily leaving for a visit to the stables at Sandringham in the rain.*

Right *Evening-gowned and back in London, Her Majesty comes to the Royal Albert Hall for the British Legion Festival of Remembrance.*

However dear her memories may be, however, Her Majesty has never buried herself in nostalgia. Forward-looking, she likes to see brightness in the future. So she must surely approve of the young people of the new generations of 'Royals' who, unburdened by State responsibilities, are now emerging into adult life and moulding themselves to earn their livings in the world outside palace walls – something unknown in former days. Grandson Viscount Linley, son of Princess Margaret and the Earl of Snowdon, (a separated couple of parents but equally proud of the boy), is a good example. He is in business. He began by running a workshop of his own in Dorking, Surrey, as a fully trained craftsman in wood, a maker of beautifully carved furniture. And his sister, Lady Sarah Armstrong-Jones, is bent on being a career girl, without 'pulling rank'. She is artistic too. Once boarding school was over, she won a place for herself as a day pupil at a School of Arts and Crafts in South London.

Princess Alexandra's children are determined to earn their livings; and that is the aim of the sons and daughter of the Duke and Duchess of Kent too.

Even in the immediate Royal Family, the reigning Queen's own children, young Prince Edward – probably the most studious of his generation, having emerged from Gordonstoun bearing some hopeful A-Level passes, and with university in his sights – showed the trend by going overseas for two terms as a schoolteacher-coach in New Zealand. Ultimately he may take up a Service career like his brothers. He has had his eye on the Royal Marines, and learned to fly during a Royal Air Force course, but he may still follow a family tradition at some future time and join the Royal Navy. Admiration of the prowess of his extrovert brother, Prince Andrew, who as a Fleet Air Arm helicopter pilot was fully on active service in the 1982 Falklands campaign, could have lasting effect.

Admiration does not mean imitation, however. Edward is not

Opposite, top Youngest grandson Prince Edward shares in the senior patron's enjoyment of the 1982 Badminton Horse Trials.

Opposite, bottom An impulsive cockney salute from a meat porter to London's 'Queen Mum' on tour in Smithfield Market, 1982.

Right Viscount Linley, Princess Margaret's son – now a craftsman in wood – admires another artist's creation.

Below Prince Andrew with his grandmother, who is visiting RAF Leeming where he did part of his R.N flying training.

Above *The christening in 1942 of Prince Michael, younger son of the Duke and Duchess of Kent, was attended by a large group of European royalty. (Front row, left to right) Princess Elizabeth, Lady Patricia Ramsay, Queen Elizabeth, Prince Edward of Kent, Queen Mary, Princess Alexandra, the Duchess of Kent with the infant Prince Michael, the Dowager Marchioness of Milford Haven, Crown Princess Marthe of Norway, Princess Margaret and Princess Helena Victoria. (Back row) Princess Marie Louise, Prince Bernhard of the Netherlands, King George VI, the Duke of Kent, King Haakon of Norway, King George of the Hellenes and Crown Prince Olav of Norway.*

Left *Forty years on – Sub-Lieutenant Prince Andrew, a helicopter pilot in the Falklands campaign, steps ashore with a fellow crewman from* Invincible.

natural headline fodder – as his brother became in October, 1982, after returning from the South Atlantic. He began his leave by going on holiday to Mustique island in the Caribbean with a party of lively young people, including a twenty-five-year-old American-born actress named Koo Stark. When Prince Andrew went off to that brief West Indian holiday he flew out from England with the girl – and the world's Press flew into near-hysteria.

It is unlikely that Edward will emulate his brother's much-reported private exploits of that time, Edward being a calmer, self-contained character – though in his own quiet way as handsome and attractive as the more boisterous Andrew.

But whatever Prince Edward does in the future, he will (as his grandmother may well have reminded him) as a monarch's son have royal functions to carry out as well as following personal interests and occupations. That goes for Prince Andrew also. Princess Anne, because of her inclinations and because she has three brothers and an infant great-nephew ahead of her in the Succession, may not be so prominent. But Her Royal Highness, for one thing, has her duties as Chancellor of London University, and in these will be publicised. Her own character may also, from time to time, continue to attract news media pressure. A royal young lady – and a fine royal horsewoman – with a lot of courage and a mind and strong will of her own, has sometimes had 'a bad Press'. She has been ill-treated by intrusive cameramen or scandal-seeking gossip columnists – and has given them the rough edge of her tongue.

But when the road of official duty lies ahead, the Princess takes it with unique vigour. For instance, in the late autumn of 1982 she carried out an unusual and exacting three-week journey through eight African and Middle East countries as President of The Save the Children Fund. She flew to South Africa and then went on to Swaziland and Zimbabwe, Malawi and Kenya. After that, she entered Somalia and – despite British Foreign Office anxiety – penetrated primitive refugee camps, experiencing their pathetic scenes and challenging problems in what had recently been the Ogaden war zones on the disputed Ethiopian borders. Then followed Djibouti, in the Gulf of Aden, and North Yemen, with a stopover at Jeddah. And finally to Beirut, the war-devastated capital of Lebanon, where over-worked staffs of The Save the Children Fund and the men and women and children scraping an existence amid the ruins of buildings were in turn astonished and encouraged and delighted to see a real live princess – headscarf and stout shoes and all – desperately interested and clearly moved as she travelled amongst them. Feuding gunmen were still at their evil work not far away as she toured. Anne was in danger as well as discomfort.

This was no traditional Royal Tour. We saw a Princess being very much her mother's daughter, angry at spasmodic official attempts at over-protectiveness when she was on a dedicated and determined series of personal inspections on behalf of a world organisation. The Beirut call, unscheduled and unexpected, was typical of a deep sense of duty and understanding which Anne has several times shown, confounding her critics.

That whole strenuous tour by Princess Anne in 1982 must have gladdened the heart and excited the admiration of her grandmother. It was just the sort of exacting and successful journey that the Queen Mother had made again and again in her own years of world travel.

Much of Princess Anne's time, however, has been spent with her own family and in England, in very different surroundings from those of ravaged urban Lebanon. She inclines to pursuits which are not royal and not official: in short, to the Cotswold home where she and her husband have firmly established at Gatcombe Park a busy centre of horse-training and farming.

Perhaps, after all, she has something in common with her Aunt Margaret, though that Princess belongs to the city lights rather than the countryside. Princess Margaret, though she can and does grace a formal event impeccably, has often shown however that in her personal activities she is a law unto herself

and does not feel the need to spend her life 'being royal'. She is quick and witty, probably the most volatile, unpredictable, and essentially the most artistic member of a close-knit Royal Family.

Of them all, Prince Charles is of course most important, for the monarchial future lies with him. He is important to this book also, if only because he has always had a rare special relationship with the book's subject. Queen Elizabeth and this Number One Grandson are instinctively 'on the same wavelength' in very many things.

It must be fascinating for the Queen Mother to notice how personal emphasis has been subtly changing within the family. Because he is Heir to the Throne, and now a confident married man beginning a family of his own, the position of the Prince of Wales can be seen as gradually superseding that of his father, the Duke of Edinburgh, as chief royal male (which is not to deny that Prince Philip is First Gentleman of the realm and is, without exaggeration, one of the most able, quick-minded and restlessly energetic human beings among the leaders of public life in Britain – a real Mountbatten).

There is no need in these pages to dilate on Prince Charles as a public figure and popular person. He is a man of his times, vigorously alive to the problems and the pleasures of the Eighties. When he calls himself 'a bit of a square', he really means that – like the Queen Mother – he believes in standards and traditions, maintains faith in Britain and the Commonwealth, and has a strong sense of duty and heredity – leavened by a manifest sense of humour and ability to laugh at himself. He is experienced now in matters of State, but is the last person in the world to be wanting his mother, whom he admires

Right *Princess Anne made a hazardous tour of African and Middle Eastern countries in 1982, as President of The Save the Children Fund – a mission which appealed to her grandmother's heart. Here she is at a welfare centre in a war-torn Beirut, Lebanon.*

165

enormously, to 'move over' and let him reign. Sovereigns do not retire, certainly not exceptional ones like Queen Elizabeth II, and thirty years on the Throne is but a milestone along the path of service – that is his view; he sees himself as Heir for a long time yet, albeit with plenty to do.

The next decade may well see the Prince and Princess of Wales, giving prime support to the Queen Regnant in her work, as two 'vice presidents' for the Head of the Firm.

Meanwhile, Prince Charles, possessing that special bond with Queen Elizabeth The Queen Mother which has existed ever since he was a child, is his grandmother's foremost devotee. He understands her completely and is not at all surprised that hers is the longest-running royal fan-club. He knows better than anyone the answers to the 'how-does-she-do-it?' questions which are asked by millions of people as an enchanting life flows strongly on. One main answer is that the lady's public face and her private face are the same – the person the world knows is the person the family knows. Grannie does not put on an act. It is factual reporting, not fawning, to say that nobody sees her cross or sour, and that she genuinely is 'nice all the way through', whether trailing a cloud of glory or a chain of corgis. She is the genuine article. A national glow-worm that never stops glowing.

Who else, at the age of eighty-one, would have gone to Northern Ireland in sniper hazard to see her serving soldiers, the Queen's Dragoon Guards whose Colonel-in-Chief she is? Who else, a few weeks later, when her helicopter had to make an emergency landing and decant her onto the grass in the middle of Windsor Great Park, would have marched off, as she did, to find a small fixed-wing aircraft to give her a lift to one of the Cinque Ports 'dates' in Kent to which, as the official Warden, she is nowadays committed? Having thus managed the journey

to the coast, who but she, after what ought to have been an unnerving experience, would have unhesitatingly hopped into another 'chopper' to carry on and catch up with her Kentish engagements that same long day?

As Lord Warden of the Ports, it was she who in the same week gave imaginative welcome to returning heroes of the Falklands liberation battles. Being on board the *Britannia* for official duties along the south coast, she saw to it that, sailing from Dover to Portsmouth, she diverted the Royal Yacht to stand off The Needles and make rendezvous in the West Solent, with the liner *Queen Elizabeth 2*, converted to a troopship and bringing home survivors of naval vessels sunk in the South Atlantic conflict. It was a unique greeting, from a grateful Queen to a *Queen* of the sea, when the two vessels rode the waterway together for a few memorable moments as the trooper pressed on and the men at her crowded rails saw Her Majesty close and clear, waving her welcome-back from the deck of the royal ship.

That was one of a thousand specially remembered glimpses of her we have had through the years, a typical spontaneous happening, a signpost to the sort of woman she is.

'Legend in her lifetime' is not a bromide when it so properly fits Her Majesty. Inevitably, the stories of her quickness and her quirks too, her courage and calmness, fun and foibles, have accumulated in the recollections of friends and family. To tell some of them discloses facets of her nature. She does not 'flap', for instance. There is a remarkable illustration of the fact.

The incident which shocked an almost disbelieving world in the summer of 1982 – involving a man who managed to enter the Queen's bedroom at Buckingham Palace: an incident which queried 'Royal Security' in the headlines of every newspaper – recalled an alarming intrusion of extraordinary similarity which

Opposite *Walking back to Sandringham House after attending church service in 1969. Prince Charles is his grandmother's escort.*

Above *Princess Margaret rides out with her mother from Buckingham Palace, to witness the Trooping the Colour ceremony of June 1981 – the Sovereign's Birthday spectacle on Horse Guards Parade.*

Right *Quintessence of royalty and radiance – a summertime Queen Elizabeth amongst her flowers.*

the Queen Mother suffered forty years before. She was Queen Consort then, and the Second World War was raging. Her Majesty was at Windsor Castle one evening and, alone in her room, about to dress to go down to dinner. A wild-eyed man leaped out from behind a curtain, flung himself on the floor and gripped her by the ankles. The Queen stood stockstill. Telling of the shock afterwards, she said she realized that the attacker was in a dangerously emotional state and would probably have harmed her if she had screamed (he was in fact a temporary daytime workman at the Castle who had managed to remain hidden, after hours, because of a series of security oversights). He poured out words incomprehensively to Her Majesty for a few moments and then released his grip. The Queen quietly said 'Tell me about it,' and walked slowly across the room to press a bell. In a torrent of talk, it emerged from the man that he was a

deserter from the army and wanted to tell the Queen that 'the end had come.' His whole family, it appeared, had been killed in air raids. What violence, if any, he intended or what he imagined he could make the Queen do was not clear as he babbled on. Her Majesty remained still, listening and stifling her nervousness, until help came and the stowaway was led off. 'I was sorry for him,' she said later. 'He really meant no harm.'

She seems never to have been angry or upset about things which happen to *her*. But anxiety for other people, yes. As in the oft-repeated story about an accredited press photographer (one of my own comrades-in-arms on many a royal tour) who, one day when he was on his lawful occasions covering one of the Queen Mother's engagements, was pushed out of her path by a self-important, peremptory official. Tempers flared. Her Majesty, who knows a cameraman's business when she sees it,

Left *Leaving St Paul's after the Falklands Remembrance Service, July 26, 1982. The Queen Mother is escorted by the Prince and Princess of Wales.*

Above *At The Royal Variety Show, 1980, with Danny Kaye, Larry Hagman and Mary Martin.*

Right *Fashion-plate Lady meets a rock-fan of the Eighties dressed in heavy-metal fashion. Her Majesty, in July, 1982, was visiting young people on adventure training courses at St Katherine's Dock. The youth had strapped on all his studded leather gear for the occasion.*

immediately noticed what had happened and, turning calmly and smiling sweetly upon the Little-Hitler, said 'Please don't do that. Mr So-and-So and I are old friends.' Not unnaturally, hard-boiled Fleet Street hands are devoted to her. You see her as a pin-up on the walls of photographers' dens.

Stage people love her too. She is the star of the evening at any theatre she visits. When she attends the great charity event, the Royal Variety Performance, audiences as well as performers keep a delighted eye on the figure in the Royal Box. The performers, as a matter of fact, have a rule that *they* must not play to the royal patron, or even turn to her, except for one bow at the end of the act. Some find it hard to keep to that ration.

I remember a Royal Variety night when the late Maurice Chevalier was one of the stars, an evergreen seventy-three year old then. At the end of his marvellous fifteen-minute turn, he

brought the house down as, swinging left and away from the general audience, he went down on one knee and sang – breaking all the rules – directly to the Queen Mother sitting in the decorated Box. The song was 'You must have been a beautiful baby' and the final line he improvised that night was ''Cos, Majesty, look at you now!' The entire audience stood up and gave an ovation the like of which has rarely been heard.

They were cheering Maurice of course, but the salute was to Queen Elizabeth, who was sheer sparkle from tiara to toe. Nobody enjoys dressing-up and wearing decorations for a big event more than she does. Her gowns and gems adorn each occasion. Full-dress suits her in town and on formal duty (as tweeds do when she's off-stage and in the country), and she has an unashamed gift for tasteful glitter. Though not instrinsically interested in gems (or erratic dress fashions), she knows her jewellery, and could if she wished extravagantly indulge whims on what to wear. Once she did just that.

It was on a day during a State Visit some years ago: the King and Queen of Greece were guests. Not wishing to be outshone by anyone, the Queen Mother decided – on the day – that she would like to wear the famous Koh-i-noor diamond, the thousand-year-old monster gem from India, at a State banquet that night. This magnificent stone – called Mountain of Light, and given to Queen Victoria in 1850 by the East India Company – is not among Her Majesty's personal possessions, but is one of the Crown Jewels kept closely guarded in the Tower of London. It had, however, been one of the diamonds set in the Crown specially made for her at the 1937 Coronation. It is removable from the Crown. Very well, on that night Her Majesty wished it to be removed – from the Tower! She would wear the Koh-i-noor in her tiara at the banquet.

Her staff embarked on a torrent of frantic signals between Clarence House and the surprised Governor and Keeper of the Jewel House at Her Majesty's Tower. Nothing was easy; but messages were dispatched, documents of responsibility signed, doors unlocked. The jewel was boxed and at length sent with an escort to the Queen Mother's home, where the huge diamond was placed under guard whilst Her Majesty began to consider dressing for the evening's grand dinner.

When it came to the point, she did not wear it. She had changed her mind.

'*Plus ca change, plus c'est la memsahib,*' as Ogden Nash once parodied. Change of mind is a woman's prerogative; and discarding a fabulous jewel at the last minute certainly was a right royal prerogative. An odd and isolated incident. Her Majesty does not make a habit of demanding Crown Jewels. She does, though, at times exercise the privilege and habit of making personal decisions at the last moment. She would not upset the carefully prepared schedule of an official engagement, but does quite often like to leave to a late stage various decisions in her personal life. The suspense is a little pleasure she keeps in her own hands.

Opposite With Prince Charles and Princess Anne on the terrace of Royal Lodge in April 1954. A prized picture from the family album.

Right 'She's all right!' This picture brought universal sighs of relief. The Queen Mother emerges from hospital in December 1982 after an emergency operation for the removal of a fish-bone from her throat which had been choking her – and caused world alarm.

The legend that she is incorrigibly unpunctual has not much substance to it. It would horrify her to be like Queen Alexandra was: King Edward VII grew so despairing at having to wait for his wife to appear and go with him to a State function that he ordered all the clocks at Sandringham to be put half an hour fast.

There is nothing like that about Queen Elizabeth. She may joke about a coming event's minute-by-minute timing when her Private Secretary sets the programme before her on the desk, but she will not wilfully keep official hosts waiting. What I think Her Majesty has, rather, is a built-in resistance to being told 'It's time to set off.' It is against her nature to be rushed. The experienced lady-in-waiting probably allows for the 'oh-dear-are-we-late?' delay of a minute or two which her mistress has sometimes seemed teasingly to engender and innocently to enjoy. And the driver of the royal car may find that he has fewer minutes to get from point 'A' to point 'B' than the timetable says. Occasionally he may be bidden by a ringing royal voice from the back seat to drive carefully, but more often Queen Elizabeth will happily tell her chauffeut to put on speed: she has never herself driven a car and, as a passenger, rides blissfully unconscious of the hazards of modern roads.

In this and other respects, the Queen Mother, as a royal person and one who has been a Queen for a long time, is in the nature of things a special case, spared many of the anxieties and travails that beset ordinary mortals. It is the fortune of Royalty not to know the irritations of bus queues in the rain, the lugging of bulging suitcases towards a maddening wait at Heathrow or Gatwick airports. The lady is lucky, and knows it.

Which is not to say that she is a self-indulgent individual. On

the contrary, she is essentially considerate and caring. When she helps, which is often, there are no half measures about it. Friends and staff know of thousands of unsung acts of practical kindness, privately undertaken to people and organisations – far beyond formal patronage. She has often repeated the precept instilled into a young Elizabeth Lyon by her mother: 'Work is your *devoir*, the rent you pay for life.' So she is for ever busy, and most of the time busy for other people.

The point perhaps is that the Queen Mother's sheer work is not paraded – and probably not fully appreciated because she *enjoys* being busy and wears a light-heartedness of manner in whatever she does in public or in private. That sense of fun is never far beneath the surface. She has a straightforwardness and unpretentiousness, even delight in firing a small shock at anyone in her company who is over-formal.

She has never been a slave to solemnity. A story which brings her to life and warms one to her is recounted by a lady who was with her at her home one after-lunch when Her Majesty and a few guests were chatting and at the same time looking rather casually at the television set. A public event was being relayed through 'the Box'. Suddenly, the National Anthem was played, its strains flowing out into the drawing-room. One guest half-rose to his feet. 'Oh, do switch the set off,' said the royal hostess. 'You know, unless one is actually there, it's out of place and embarrassing – like hearing the Lord's Prayer whilst playing Canasta.'

The high spirits of the Queen Mother, the stimulation of her company, make a thread which stretches far through her years. One delightful recollection, from the time when she was Queen Consort, shows her, as always, 'quick on the uptake', even in foreign languages. It concerns France (the country she most

loves to visit nowadays), or, rather, one of France's statesmen of former and darker years: Edouard Daladier, one-time Premier, the man who, with Chamberlain, signed the notorious Munich Agreement with Hitler in 1938. It was before then that Daladier was being officially entertained on a visit to Britain. Queen Elizabeth was one of those with him as he was being taken round and shown historic documents in Windsor Castle library. Daladier, whose English was peculiar, recognized one legal parchment and, pleased with himself, declared 'Yes! abiocobus!' The ejaculation was incomprehensible to the conducting party, who assumed it to be some Gallic incantation. But it was clear at once to the Queen, whose French in any case is perfect, and who replied '*Ah oui, Monsieur,*' and continued a twinkling conversation with the visitor in his own language. Only later did she enlighten the rest of the party by telling them that 'abiocobus' meant Habeas Corpus (the ancient writ concerning rights of prisoners). One wonders, incidentally, whether Daladier remembered seeing this original Act in an English castle when later he himself was a political prisoner of Hitler's Germans.

There is something very fitting that charters of justice and morality should be enshrined within the walls of Windsor, the place to which the Queen Mother has always been deeply attached. During the ruinous bombings brought by Hitler's war in was her hope that, whatever might be shattered in London, the Castle would still stand. As she prayed for the nation and a free people's survival, her prayers for Windsor were not something selfish. They were deeply symbolic.

One uses the word 'prayer' guardedly and yet advisedly in attempting any profile of Her Majesty. She is unquestionably a Christian of firm belief and trust. Church attendances are not,

Opposite *The royal gesture which all the world knows. Queen Elizabeth acknowledging the cheers of the crowd at the gate of her London home. A birthday picture before the traditional family luncheon.*

Below *The working Queen Mother, here seen at her desk at Clarence House in London.*

to her, formalities. Her faith – she would prefer that to '*her religion*' – is not ostentatious, and is rooted in moral truths that, in her own words, 'do not alter with a changing world.' Too comprehending and tolerant to be a 'churchwoman' in any narrow sense, she instinctively respects the religions of others. She would not feel awkward in a mosque (I don't think she would feel awkward anywhere), and in her own land is as much at home when going to worship in a small Presbyterian chapel as in the grand Royal Peculiar which we know as Westminster Abbey.

Hers is a morality which transcends sectarian divisions. It is also, essentially, something private, not a subject for glib chat. Indeed, in this and many other things, the Queen Mother is – for all the social shine of her – in a sense a *secret* person who will hug to herself her beliefs and hopes. She much needs, I think, her times of privacy, some solitudes. Such requirements would be a natural complement to the demanding pull of her official life spent in publicity's spotlights.

So she is not given to broadcasting her personal opinions on today's seething world, though such a sensitive person must have strong, and in her case perhaps inflexible, views. She can hardly be indifferent on such subjects as battered babies, Soccer louts, squabbling Churchmen, destructive Marxists, Hobson's Choice

Opposite *The Lady of Clarence House surrounded by flowers and books in the privacy of her London home.*

Below *As the public has so often seen her – she watches Princess Anne on Doublet at Badminton. This was in April 1971.*

schooling, trades union dictators and shop-floor scrimshanking, mob violence, rising terrorism, mindless strikes in industry which are gobbledygooked as 'withdrawal of labour'. She would never say 'These things can't be helped.' There is no joy in them, and she *wants* to help.

As a compassionate person herself, she is saddened by the hardships of the unemployed – especially the school-leavers earnestly seeking jobs – and is acutely concerned over the dangers which world economic depression brings. She does in fact give unpublicised support to organisations working to alleviate suffering and to uphold the best in British character. She shares today's national fears and frustrations, for indifference has no part in her make-up. That is why countless charities and good causes have attracted her generous heart and purse. She is a human being of impulse and emotion.

Not that sorrow or temper ever *show* in this lady. Her own standards, manifest in her conduct and glow of personality, are a shield as well as a strength. Nobody would dream of calling Queen Elizabeth 'The Iron Lady'. But she, who was an Empress and – quite apart from that – long ago evolved well-tried codes by which to abide, is by nature and experience conservative, with a small 'C'. Although the best listener in the world to other people's views, and quite often privately a helper of campaigns which may not necessarily have precisely her own rules and ways, is never likely to be blown off her established course. It would indeed be a brave man who attempted to make her change her opinions, some of which are unashamedly dated and have not altered since she shared them with the King very many years ago. Perhaps fervent emotion has always overridden

Opposite *Delight all round as Grannie holds five-month-old Prince Andrew in the garden of Clarence House. It was Her Majesty's sixtieth birthday.*

Right *Celebrating her seventy-fifth birthday on August 4, 1975 at Royal Lodge. Prince Andrew, on the right, has just presented a gift of two pottery dishes he had made at Gordonstoun, his school.*

political acumen. It would be very hard indeed to cavil at that.

It is hard to cavil *at all*, try as perhaps you might, with a person who seems never to have had an ugly thought in her head. The courtesy and those beautiful manners are bewitching, and are so infectious that it is difficult to imagine anybody in her orbit being graceless or unpleasant – at least not when she's watching! She is herself a *good* person, and expects others to be so. She is slow to censure, loth to believe that this or that individual may be substandard or corrupt. But, if convinced, she is firmly and forever unforgiving to those who prove harmfully disloyal and 'let the side down'.

No doubt she is fortunate in that she is active, wanted, and in full employment. She is thankful for that, even though she has never been anything else *but* busy and never known the dejection of idleness or the drag of the hours that comes to those without a hobby. It happens that her work is her hobby, pleasantness her business and the secret of her success. If a member of her staff should make bold to suggest that perhaps now she might now ease-up a little, the reply will be: 'But I *enjoy* what I am and what I'm doing.'

So she still has a full diary. When great organisations are planning their centenaries or inaugurations, the first question at the first planning meeting is quite likely to be: 'I wonder if we could get The Queen Mother to come?' If eventually she does accept the invitation and does come, it is a good bet that at some moment she will momentarily upset the programme – in the nicest way. Slipping through the front line-up of directors and managers she will have an unscheduled word with the pushed-back phalanx of typists and liftboys who never thought they'd get even a good look at her.

That is the lady's golden touch, the common touch, which has been such a gift to Throne and people. And still is.

Her personality, and the pattern of each year – Windsor, Sandringham, London, Scotland – with its scores of engagements, vocational and social, all this is resolutely unaltered. Retirement from highest office in London's University and reduced numbers of visits to overseas countries of the Commonwealth have eased the pressure a little, but requests for Her Majesty's presence all over the United Kingdom (and amongst her Scots in Canada) mean continuance of eventful days.

Inevitably, recent years have dealt saddening blows by the passing of old friends and loved contemporaries; but with the Queen Mother it is a point of honour never to wear grief upon one's sleeve. The sorrow is within her private self; and, with an uplift of the chin, she will say 'Life must go on' – and, for her, life is fulfilling duties, a stimulating involvement with people and events.

So, our Queen Elizabeth The Queen Mother is radiant as ever. Her 'fans' will look forward to her ninetieth birthday. The timeless elegance, the genuine grace and goodness so welcome in an era of meretricious trivialities, the wish to work on and on, the evidence of a Stuart wit and charm (no dark Hanoverian genes!) – all this is with us still.

It would be a very insensitive visitor to Clarence House in these middle-Eighties who did not warm to the smiling figure coming forward in greeting, a broad-shouldered, five-foot-two, slim-waisted lady with eyes like blue lights, complexion creamy and with no excessive make-up, holding herself well, speaking with a light voice that is clear as a bell, and making those typically expressive gestures of the hands. It would be a very poor memory that did not retain a picture of Her Majesty at work in the south-west corner of her big first-floor room overlooking the garden, sitting with her back to the light of the windows at a large mahogany desk loaded with filing trays and family photographs, a sunny executive, brightly dressed and busy with her papers and her letters and her telephones.

The room is full of pictures of her children, her grandchildren, and now her great-grandchildren. And all about her, in that and the other rooms and corridors of the big house, the beautiful furnishings and mementos, reminders of her life's story, portraits of her ancestors, and many a photograph of the man she loved and married and lost so soon.

Long-widowed now, she has come to occupy, simply by her own outgoing qualities, a golden niche in the temple of fame and a lustrous strand in the fabric of the century. The special aura about her is something no other one person possesses. She is – and this is no hyperbole – an extraordinary woman, and her status is recognized nationally and internationally, cherished in hearts and homes as well as in history books, transcending class and creed.

The facts of her unique position came startlingly into world focus through a sudden scare one night in November, 1982, when during dinner at Royal Lodge a fish-bone stuck in the Queen Mother's throat and threatened to choke her. No expedient by her family or local doctor brought relief, and she was rushed to a London hospital in the early hours for the removal of the obstruction, under a general anaesthetic. Happily, the extraction was smoothly done and the patient 'came round' with the resilience of a youngster. Little more than twenty-four hours later, Her Majesty, smartly dressed and smiling, emerged from the hospital door and, with a pause and a wave for the multitude of waiting cameramen, nipped into her car and was driven home. Her staff, though accustomed to her resilience, described her as 'bubbly, quite amazing'.

The incident proved yet again her marvellously strong constitution. But, more than that, the public reaction which the incident evoked, the anxiety and the prayers, was a measure of the affection in which this Queen Elizabeth is held. For several hours, whilst newspaper headlines cried: 'Queen Mum – Emergency Operation', the nation held its breath and waited for every bulletin.

It was prayer for a human being who is also an institution: she is no linchpin of a Government or Officer of State. The love and the fear which sprang so immediately to life was because of the service she has given to Britain and because of the sort of person she specially is – the stuff of aunties who are favourites and grans who are fun. It would be odd if she didn't *know* that she is widely popular; and indeed the many official tokens of that are treasured. But dearer to her than the Loyal Addresses and Freedoms of Cities, I suspect, are the spontaneously earthy tributes of ordinary people such as the one paid by a London taxi driver when he learned one day that his passenger was going to tea with the Lady of Clarence House: 'Cor, sir! Lucky you! She's a great old stick!'

A genuine salute. But words more fitting to her story and her style must end this book, a tribute to a unique lady of the Royal House, who for so very many years has proved the great worth of bringing native, non-royal blood into the dynasty – and royalty into the light of common day. Many of literature's famous descriptions of wonderful women would be apposite, but one Shakespeare garland is eminently her due:

Age cannot wither her, nor custom stale
Her infinite variety.

Opposite December 22, 1977. Five generations at the Buckingham Palace christening of Peter, Princess Anne's infant son – the eldest being the late Princess Alice, Countess of Athlone (seated beside Princess Anne), a grandchild of Queen Victoria. The paternal grandparents, Mr and Mrs Peter Phillips, are on the left.

Below At Westminster Abbey yet again – a day of indelible memories for the subject of this book. In December 1982 Queen Elizabeth presented a special Children of Courage award to thirteen youngsters. The girl on the left is blind, yet swims, rides and cycles. She could not see the royal smile but the glow of the Special Lady's personality will remain with her.

Photographic Acknowledgements

The illustrations on the following pages are reproduced by Gracious Permission of Her Majesty the Queen: 22 left, 22 right, 25, 26 top, 33 bottom, 37 top, 42 bottom, 59 right, 61 top, 68 top, 68 bottom.

COLOUR

B.B.C. Hulton Picture Library, London 110 top; BIPNA, London 131 top; Camera Press, London: Jim Bennett 155; Camera Press: Patrick Lichfield 132–3; Camera Press: Norman Parkinson 173; Colour Library International, London 153, 154 bottom; Lord Adam Gordon 47 top; Tim Graham, London 131 bottom, 174; Captain R. Grimshaw 46–47; Hamlyn Group Picture Library 2, 19, 20 top, 20 bottom, 45, 46 top, 46 bottom, 48, 65, 66, 67, 68 top, 68 bottom, 77 top, 77 bottom, 78 top, 78 bottom, 87, 88, 89 top, 89 bottom, 90 top, 90 bottom, 175, 176; John Scott, Bracknell 99, 100 top, 100 bottom, 109, 110 bottom, 111 top, 111 bottom, 112, 121 top, 121 bottom, 122, 143 top, 143 bottom, 144 top, 144 bottom, 156; Syndication International, London 134, 154 top.

BLACK AND WHITE

Aerofilms, Boreham Wood 136; Associated Newspapers, London 106, 119, 123, 124; Associated Press, London 107; B.B.C. Hulton Picture Library, London 34 top, 34 bottom, 36 left, 38, 44, 53, 58 bottom, 63, 76 top, 76 bottom, 82 bottom, 83 bottom, 84 top, 93 top, 141 bottom, 170; BIPNA, London 118, 125, 126 top, 126 bottom; Camera Press, London 11 top, 27 top, 64, 69 top, 72 bottom, 74, 93 bottom, 152 top, 180; Camera Press: Peter Abbey 10 bottom, 114; Camera Press: Cecil Beaton 172; Camera Press: Jim Bennett 127 left, 127 right; Camera Press: Alan Davidson 128, 129, 135 top, 163 bottom; Camera Press: Norman Parkinson 116, 167 bottom, 179; Camera Press: Richard Slade 162 top; Camera Press: The Times 13, 130; Camera Press: Alex Wilson 115 left; Central Press, London 11 bottom, 26 bottom, 29 bottom, 31, 32 top, 32 bottom, 33 top, 43, 64, 72 top, 75 bottom, 86, 94 bottom, 103 top, 105 top, 147 top, 158, 166, 178; Express Newspapers, London 10 top; Tim Graham, London 117, 160; Major John Griffin 82 top; Hamlyn Group Picture Library 14, 15, 17 top, 17 bottom, 18 top, 18 bottom, 24, 29 top, 30, 36 right, 40 bottom, 54, 59 left, 60, 61 bottom, 138, 139 bottom, 140, 141 top, 147 bottom, 157 bottom, 164 top, Keystone Press Agency, London 42 top, 51 top, 52, 55, 58 top, 72–73, 79 bottom, 83 top, 91 bottom, 92, 98 bottom, 103 bottom, 145 bottom, 146, 148, 150 top left, 159, 177; Popperfoto, London 27 bottom, 28 top, 35, 37 bottom, 39, 40 top, 41 bottom, 49, 50, 51 bottom, 56, 69 bottom, 70 top, 70 bottom, 71, 79 top, 85 top, 85 bottom, 96 top, 97, 142, 145 top, 150 top right, 150 bottom, 151 top; Press Association, London 28 bottom, 101, 120, 137, 164 bottom, 167 top; The Save the Children Fund, London 165; John Scott, Bracknell 75 top; Sport & General Press Agency, London 151 bottom; Syndication International, London 9, 12, 41 top, 80, 94 top, 95, 96 bottom, 98 top, 102, 104, 105 bottom, 108 top, 108 bottom, 113 top, 113 bottom, 115 right, 135 bottom, 152 bottom, 157 top, 161, 162 bottom, 163 top, 168–9, 169 top, 169 bottom, 171, 181; The Times, London 62; Windsor Archives 22 left, 22 right, 25, 26 top, 33 bottom, 37 top, 42 bottom, 59 right, 61 top.